Paul's Letters to Local Churches

Paul's Letters

TO LOCAL CHURCHES

Francis Gerald Ensley

BISHOP, THE METHODIST CHURCH, THE DES MOINES AREA

ABINGDON PRESS
New York • *Nashville*

Bible quotations in this book are from the Revised Standard Version of the Bible, copyright 1952, and are used by permission of the National Council of Churches of Christ in the United States of America, owner of the copyright. The King James Bible (Authorized Version) has been used in a few exceptions. Reference to the King James Bible is indicated by the use of A.V. following the quotation.

CONTENTS

INTRODUCTION

THE APOSTLE PAUL did not know that Methodist women would be studying his letters in 1956-57! If he had, he would doubtless have shaped them into a form more suitable for study. The fact that he did not lays upon his interpreter a twofold responsibility. First, he must express the implications of Paul's message for the world today. Paul was a man of the first century. As we shall see, he did not anticipate that there would even be a world in 1956. Both his message and his language require translation to bring their fullest meaning to twentieth-century readers. I have endeavored to be faithful to Paul's intent, though the phrasing in which I have presented it is contemporary. I have used (with very few exceptions) the text of the recent translation, the Revised Standard Version.

Secondly, the Apostle's interpreter must reorganize his material. Paul sometimes wrote, as we sometimes write to intimate friends, in a white heat of feeling. The words bubbled out, not always in logical order. Often he treated the same idea in widely-scattered portions of his work. I have tried to bring together for this study material which seems to belong together, related ideas from various sections of the letters to the Ephesians and Colossians, the Romans, the Corinthians, the Thessalonians, the Philippians, and the letter to Philemon, because their contents are closely related in subject matter. The ideas are Paul's; I have only supplied a string for the bundles.

It is impossible fully to acknowledge my indebtedness. My creditors are many. The content of this book is Paul's life and thought passed through the prism of contemporary scholarship. A host of New Testament students have contributed to our knowledge. For the inspiration to study Paul I am under obligation to no one more than to an old friend and teacher, Doctor William Jackson Lowstuter, who infected so many generations of men at Boston University School of Theology with his enthusiasm for the Apostle. I should like to think that a tithe of his inspiration might overflow into this little book.

F. G. E.

I

THE MAN PAUL

Paul, the great apostle to the Gentiles, was, after Jesus, the mightiest single force in shaping our Christian religion. He it was who tore Christianity loose from Judaism, giving the Christian community the consciousness of being followers of a new religion. By his missionary labor he transplanted Christianity from Palestine to the soil of Europe, into the culture of Greece and Rome. He is the immediate author of at least nine books of the New Testament and the source of four more, while Acts devotes seventeen chapters to his life and every other Christian writing of the first century feels his power.

Paul was the first Christian theologian; the Lutheran, Presbyterian, and Reformed churches stem directly from him. He is of peculiar interest to Methodists because it was while John Wesley listened to the reading of Luther's *Preface to the Commentary on the Epistle to the Romans* that Wesley felt his heart strangely warmed. Paul's influence flows in the blood of every Christian.

His Early Life. Paul was born, perhaps two or three years after Jesus, in Tarsus, a city which boasted a famous Greek university and sat at the crossroads of Asian and Western culture in the Roman province of Cilicia. Paul was a Jew, "of the tribe of Benjamin, a Hebrew of the Hebrews" (Phil. 3:5). He grew up in a strict religious home; his father was a Pharisee (Acts 23:6), in American terms, a Puritan. He never mentions his family, though we know he had a married sister living in Jerusalem (Acts 23:16). It is not unlikely that his silence is occasioned by the fact that he broke with his proud Pharisaic family when he became a Christian.

He received his education proper in Jerusalem, where he tells us that he sat "at the feet of Gamaliel" (Acts 22:3), one of the most highly respected rabbis of the time, in order to become a rabbi himself. His training there, if it followed the customary pattern of Jewish schooling, was confined to a thorough study of the Scriptures—the Old Testament. The student's work consisted mainly of committing to memory passages from the Bible and "the tradition of the elders"—the learned men's interpretation of them. There was very little in the theological training itself to kindle the imagination, but to tread the streets of the Holy City, so rich in the dearest traditions of his people, and to worship in the Temple must have done much to redeem the arid discipline of Paul's studies.

Somewhere along the line Paul learned a trade, the weaving of goat hair into tent cloth. In so doing he complied with an old Jewish custom, which required that every lad should learn a trade, no matter what profession he might ultimately pursue. Gamaliel, his theological teacher, is credited with saying that "learning of any kind unaccompanied by a trade ends in nothing and leads to sin."

When he came of age Paul probably married, according to the custom of his people who still set great store by family life, although he never refers to his wife. When, in I Corinthians, he counsels on marriage, he reveals too great a knowledge of the intimacies of married life to have been a theorizing bystander. Yet he does not seem to have had a wife at the time he wrote his letters, perhaps in his late fifties. Some scholars believe that he was a widower.

PAUL'S CONVERSION TO CHRISTIANITY

During Paul's early thirties Jesus of Nazareth began his world-changing ministry. Probably Paul never saw the Master in the flesh, for surely he would have used the fact to refute his enemies when they questioned his right to witness for Christ. But, if Paul never met Jesus personally, he was soon on speaking terms with his disciples. Immediately after the Crucifixion, a group of Jesus' followers made their way to Jerusalem (Acts 1:15), probably in the confidence that the Messiah, as prophecy had foretold, would soon and suddenly appear there (Malachi 3:1). Very soon, too, they were showing the breadth of spirit implicit in the gospel. They, like their Lord, had fellowship with aliens, and they set his teachings above the law. Judaism could not tolerate such a threat to its integrity and called for persecutors to put down these blasphemies. Saul, the young rabbi, joined these *vigilantes*.

He hurled himself with zeal into harassment of the new sect. But the very fever with which he pursued the Christians revealed that all was not well with his own soul. His religion taught that if he kept the Mosaic Law he would be saved. But, alas, he found that the Law let him down. It condemned him instead of redeeming him. He discovered that, try as he would, he could not keep it. As he tells us in his Letter to the Romans, the things that he wanted to do he could not, and the very things that he hated he did. And he sobbed, "Wretched man that I am, who shall deliver me from this body of death?" (Rom. 7:15, 24). Though he projected his misery, "taking it out on the Christians," he could not have failed to contrast the bitter turmoil of his soul with the calm peace, tender affections, and steadfast devotion to their Lord of the humble people whom he harried.

After witnessing the stoning of Stephen, the first Christian martyr, Paul took the assignment of going from Jerusalem up to Damascus to incite the Jews there against the fugitive Christians who had fled from suppression at Jerusalem. As he neared the Syrian city, a heavenly radiance overwhelmed him, and he believed that he saw Jesus in his risen and glorified body. See accounts in Acts 9:3-7; 22:4-11; 26:12-19; and Galatians 1:15-17. He fell to the earth, overwhelmed by his vision which left him sightless for three days.

What happened? Did Jesus appear literally in the body and speak to Paul? Or was there a mystic revelation realized within the privacy of Paul's own mind? Or did some objective happening trigger an event within—as the reading of Luther's *Preface to the Commentary on the Epistle to the Romans* at the prayer meeting in Aldersgate was unexpectedly to turn up the thermostat in Wesley's heart? We cannot say, at this distance. Who of us can "explain" his own conversion experience, let alone that of a man nineteen centuries ago?

Whatever queries we may have as to the nature of the event, there is no doubt of its life-transforming consequences. As Paul himself put it, the "old man" died; he became a "new creature" (II Cor. 5:17; A.V.). He lost his skepticism concerning the claims of Christ and believed Jesus to be Messiah. Whereas he had been a persecutor he now became an Apostle. In the place of inner division and nagging restlessness of spirit, there came the peace which truly passed all understanding. Under the blazing Syrian sun that day, Paul entered into a mystic comradeship with Christ which was to carry him bravely across the Roman Empire, through bitter persecution, and at last to a martyr-death for Jesus' sake. After all, the decisive thing is not when, where, or how we were born but that we are alive! From Damascus on, Paul knew *life*.

The blinded Paul was led to nearby Damascus, harbored by the Christian community there, and baptized by Ananias, one of the disciples. There the mists close in on Paul's activities. We have references to a stay in Arabia, perhaps to ponder the experience he had undergone. See Galatians 1:17. He returned to Damascus for a season then fled to Jerusalem by stealth when the Jewish population sought the death of this patriot-turned-renegade. A brief sojourn in Jerusalem seems to have been followed by a stay in his native Tarsus. Then came the long period of association with Barnabas in Antioch, variously estimated from one to fourteen years.

FIRST MISSIONARY EFFORTS

During Paul's residence in the great Syrian city came the call to missionary work. Whether it was an immediate summons, a product of the Damascus upheaval, or whether it was a slow, maturing conviction which grew out of his brooding over the world's need of Christ, and his observance of the appeal of the gospel to men of all nationalities in cosmopolitan Antioch, we do not know. The idea of a mission to acquaint the world with Christianity took possession of him.

FIRST MISSIONARY JOURNEY

In company with Barnabas and John Mark he made a "trial run." They crossed to the neighboring island of Cyprus, the homeland of Barnabas, and after traversing it from end to end they passed over to the southern coast of Asia Minor. Here they made short stays in the larger cities: Perga, where—to Paul's disgust—young Mark deserted the mission; Antioch in Pisidia, where they aroused great interest in Christ in the synagogues; Iconium, where converts were won; Lystra, where Paul was stoned by angry Jews and left for dead; Derbe, where many disciples were made. Then, retracing their steps, they sailed home to Antioch, leaving behind them a number of small but vigorous communities, and taking with them the conviction that the world was ripe for the proclamation of the gospel.

Upon his return from this journey, Paul ran head on into a problem which was to dog him all his days, namely, what was to be the relation of Jews and Gentiles in the Church? Until this time, it had been taken for granted that the gospel was primarily for Jews and that aliens were to be admitted to the Church only as a favor and on condition that they observed the Jewish Law. But as Paul had labored in Antioch and its Gentile environs, the conviction had dawned on him that Christianity was not a mere sect of Judaism, but a new religion, grounded on faith instead of on legal obedience. In his work among non-Jewish Christians Paul had found all the fruits of the Spirit of Christ without strict observance of the law. Further, Paul saw that insistence upon Jewish legal observances would spell the ruin of the gospel, for in effect it would dethrone Christ as the one Savior of the world and make the Law equally essential. When troublemakers came up from Jerusalem, insisting that Paul's Gentile converts undergo the Jewish rite of circumcision, he resolved to make an issue of it.

Taking his friend Barnabas, Paul went down to Jerusalem to the mother church, and engaged in controversy with James and Peter, the leaders of Jewish conservatism, in what is called "The Jerusalem Conference." After a warm, intense, but finally amicable discussion, they agreed that Paul and Barnabas should be free to present their gospel to the Gentiles, while the Law should be binding only on the Jews.

This compromise marked a milestone in the history of the Church. It cleared the way for an immediate Gentile mission. It established the timeless religious truth, later to be reaffirmed by the Protestant Reformation, that men are saved through faith, not works. It emancipated Christianity from its position as a Jewish sect and planted its feet on the high road to becoming a world religion.

APOSTLE TO THE GENTILES:
SECOND MISSIONARY JOURNEY

On the threshold of another missionary tour, Paul and Barnabas disagreed over Mark's desertion on the first journey. So Paul took Silas, a member of the Jerusalem church who had come to Antioch, and set out to revisit the churches in Cilicia. When they tried to go into Asia, they were "forbidden by the Holy Spirit" (Acts 16:6). Whatever the barrier which the missionaries interpreted as the work of the Spirit, they came to Troas, a seaport town near the site of ancient Troy. Here Paul had a most momentous vision: in a dream he saw a man from Macedonia beckoning him to come over and help (Acts 16:9). Paul concluded at once that it was God's call to preach the gospel in Greece. That day was another milestone in Christian history, for it marked the advance of the Christian faith from Asia, the home of the Jews, into Europe, the world of the Gentiles.

Philippi was the first Macedonian city in which Paul worked. There he founded a church which, as we shall see, was more warmly attached to him than any of his other churches. At Philippi, however, Paul and Silas came into conflict with powerful interests, were mobbed, thrown into prison, and were released only when they disclosed their Roman citizenship.

From Philippi Paul went on to Thessalonica, a thriving commercial city where he founded another church. But the Jews raised the cry of sedition against him, and his friends spirited him away lest he might be destroyed by violence. He proceeded by way of Beroea to Athens, renowned capital of Greece.

It was in Athens that Paul encountered his first real setback. In other cities he had been able to found churches, though troublemakers had sometimes handled him roughly. In sophisticated Athens he was invited to set forth his views, but when it was discovered that what he had to offer was not a new and interesting philosophy, but an earnest, sacrificial religion, his listeners politely brushed him off.

Deeply depressed, Paul passed on to Corinth. In that great pagan city his spirits revived when he was able to establish one of his strongest, albeit at times most unruly, churches. Paul wrote his letters to the Thessalonians from here.

Following a brief trip to Jerusalem, Paul journeyed to Ephesus where he stayed three years, laying the foundation of one of the most influential Christian communities in the Mediterranean world (Acts 19). From Ephesus he dispatched his great letters to the Galatians and the Corinthians. There, too, he met with great danger: as he says, he "fought with [wild] beasts at Ephesus" (I Cor. 15:32). Paul may literally have fought wild beasts in the Ephesian amphitheatre; he may have been using the words in a figurative sense, indicating rough treatment by a mob; or he may refer to his inner conflicts while at Ephesus.

From Ephesus Paul travelled back to Corinth, and while waiting for friends to join him he composed his famous theological treatise, the Epistle to the Romans. From Corinth Paul proceeded through Macedonia and along the coast of Asia Minor to Tyre and Caesarea with the collection he had gathered from the Gentile churches for the poor of the mother church in Jerusalem. Nothing is told of the presentation of the gift when Paul reached the capital, though under the circumstances he probably would not have been ill received.

THE LAST YEARS

While Paul was in Jerusalem, Jews from Asia Minor, who knew of his association with aliens in Antioch and Ephesus, raised the cry that the Apostle had defiled the sacred Temple by bringing Greeks into it (Acts 21:27-28). A fanatical mob gathered and would have torn him to pieces had not a detail of Roman soldiers rescued him. After a stormy appearance before the Jewish Sanhedrin, Paul was hustled off to Caesarea by the authorities who got word of a plot to lynch him (Acts 23:12-35). He languished in prison two years and then, wearying of the law's delay, and perhaps fearing that he would never get justice in the corrupt courts of Judea, he uttered the potent, "I appeal unto Caesar." To this, Festus, the Roman governor, had no alternative but to send him direct to Rome.

After a drama-filled journey, during which his ship was wrecked off Malta by an early winter storm, Paul at last reached Italy and was conducted along the Appian Way to Rome.

Paul remained a prisoner in Rome for about three years, though he was allowed considerable freedom. He lived in a house of his own, guarded by a soldier who was apparently bound to him by a chain. See Acts 28:20; Philippians 1:13; Philemon 1, 9, 10, 13; Colossians 4:3, 18; Ephesians 3:1; 4:1; and 6:20. Being imprisoned did not prevent the Apostle's discoursing with the Roman Jews (Acts 28), and he reported to the Philippians that his imprisonment had actually worked out for the advancement of the gospel (Phil. 1:12). Also, Paul found time to pen letters to the Colossians, the Ephesians, and the Philippians, as well as to write the moving missive to Philemon about his returning slave, Onesimus.

But the visible trail soon runs out. The narrative in Acts breaks off before the trial is reached, and we may conclude that it ended disastrously. One of the best-authenticated traditions of antiquity tells us that Paul was beheaded by Nero on the Ostian Way a little distance out of the city. The Cathedral of St. Paul's-Without-the-Walls marks the spot where he is said to have been buried.

PAUL'S LETTERS AND THEIR INTERPRETATION

Paul's epistles are *bona fide* letters. They were not designed as literary productions, nor even intended for publication, nor penned self-consciously with History peering over the writer's shoulder. They were personal messages that Paul wrote from a full heart to his dearest friends on their common concerns. They spring from life-situations: thanks for a gift (Phil. 4:14 ff.), the desire to cool off fanatics who were despoiling the Thessalonian Church, answers to queries on the Christian proprieties raised by the Corinthians. They were written (Rom. 16:22; II Thess. 3:17; and I Cor. 16:21) with the digressions, diffuseness, and violent turns of tone and subject matter that cling to oral compositions. They were inscribed on parchment or papyrus leaves whose originals have long since turned to dust.

The character of the letters, of course, prescribes the way they are to be read and interpreted. To understand a letter requires more than comprehension of its obvious meaning. To get the maximum from a letter requires the ability to read between the lines. It takes not only eyesight, but insight. A letter is a personal communication without the gesture and accent of face-to-face converse. The imagination of the reader has to supply the overtones of meaning which the eye and ear easily catch in direct contacts. The reader of Paul's letters, especially, must not only grasp the Apostle's palpable meaning, but have sufficient knowledge of the invisible background to put the meaning into its context. To make Paul intelligible there must be in the mind an answer ready for such queries as these regarding the membership of each church to which he writes: Why is Paul writing to this church, anyway? What are the peculiarities of this church which would actually cause this letter to differ from a communication to any other? What has the

Apostle's relationship been to this church? What assumptions is Paul making about the world and Christ and man? That is, what theology lies behind the things he writes?

Having laid hold of Paul's meaning, however, is still not enough. A young minister was shaking hands at the door the other morning after a preaching service. A very perceptive layman remarked as he passed by, "That, sir, was a wonderful sermon on Paul. It is a shame Paul could not have been present to hear it!"

There is a subtle rebuke in that observation. Sermons on Paul are not for Paul, but for us! Likewise, his letters are not just for first-century Christians. Their meanings must be translated into our own twentieth-century terms if they are to bless us.

Having grasped what Paul meant to his contemporaries, we must go on and ask: What does this counsel of his mean today? Is it still valid? Is Paul ahead of us or behind us on this issue? What difference would it make if we should accept his teachings in our churches today? What should a present-day Christian do about these teachings? Only as we raise such inquiries will the letters of this great first-century leader edify us.

II

PAUL'S IDEA OF THE CHURCH
THE BODY OF CHRIST

II

From the hour that Paul the persecutor met Christ on the Damascus road until he gave the last full measure of his devotion on the Ostian Way, the Apostle had two sovereign concerns. One was, of course, his Lord. The other was the Church. The only sin whose memory burned like fire in him was the sin which he had committed against the Church. And when you find him at his highest, jubilant and enraptured, he is thinking of the Church. Paul was one of the chief founders of the early Church, especially its Gentile branches. He painted the picture of its world mission. He framed in large part its message. As a practical administrator he wrestled with its problems. He formulated the philosophy of its nature and function. In these chapters we are to ponder Paul's contribution to the Christian Church.

As we engage in this task it is well to remember that there was a Church in existence before Paul entered the scene and that it has persisted long after he made his exit.

There was a living Christian community before he was converted to the faith. Nor does Paul speak the last word on the Church; since his day we have learned much that he never foresaw. Magnificent as it is, Paul's contribution was superimposed upon an institution already present. A word about the primitive Church may, then, be in order.

THE EARLY CHURCH

Jesus had not attempted in his lifetime to organize a Church; but a large body of believers, of whom the Twelve Disciples were the core, gathered around him. After his death about one hundred and twenty of these made their way to Jerusalem (Acts 1:15). Simon Peter was their leader. On the day of Pentecost, seven weeks after the Crucifixion, a group of believers were met together when a sudden divine impulse came upon them and they "were all filled with the Holy Spirit" (Acts 2). They received an unshakable conviction that God had given them the Spirit promised of old to his people. On that day of Pentecost the Church was born.

At first the disciples had no distinctive name. They called themselves the "brethren," the "believers," "those who waited for the coming of Jesus Christ." They were at first— indeed through most of the first century—only an informal (rather than an organized) brotherhood of Jesus' followers.

These brotherhoods differed in many ways from what we mean by "church":

1. The first Christians were faithful in attendance at the Temple and in obedience to the Mosaic Law. Their services

were held in addition to the regular Jewish observances and formed an adjunct to the Hebrew synagogues. The relationship to the Jewish congregation was comparable to that of the early Methodists to the Church of England: the services were extra, auxiliary to those of the regular religious community. The reason the Christian movement was not strangled in its cradle is that, in its crucial years, it was looked on as but a sect of the already accepted Judaism.

2. The early Christians were without buildings or equipment. They met in the homes of their more well-to-do members—Paul sometimes sends greetings to his friends "and the church in their house" (Rom. 16:5; I Cor. 16:19; and Col. 4:15)—or in public halls. Cathedrals, sanctuaries, educational units, and the elaborate paraphernalia which we associate with the Church belong to a much later time.

3. There was little formal organization in the primitive Church (Acts 6:1-6). It had no officers in the strict sense. There were leaders, of course, like Paul, the Twelve, and others who ruled by virtue of strength or personality and religious experience. Occasionally such officers as "elders," "presbyters," "deacons" are mentioned, but they were informal moral supervisors of the little Christian communities rather than the formally elected officials we have come to know under such names.

4. Groups of laymen and women carried on the work of the Christian community. While such titles as "apostles," "prophets," "teachers," and "pastors" are cited in Paul's writings, they do not refer to "ordained ministers." The persons so designated were lay individuals who exercised certain functions in the Christian community. The only

ordination they knew was a special capacity for given tasks.

5. Church life was very simple. The intricate liturgies and ceremonials of churches in our time are the product of a long process of development. One of the earliest descriptions we are given of church life is in Acts 2:42: "they devoted themselves to the apostles' teaching and fellowship, to the breaking of bread and the prayers." The apostles, those who had known Jesus, recited their memories. They prayed together. They ate common meals recalling Jesus' admonition, "Do this in remembrance of me" (I Cor. 11:24 and I Cor. 10:16-17). Through these fellowship meals our observance of the Lord's Supper has descended. This pretty well encompasses the church life in the days when Saul of Tarsus was admitted to the fellowship.

PAUL'S CONCEPTION OF THE CHURCH AS THE BODY OF CHRIST

Paul's first great service to the infant Church was in supplying it with a philosophy of existence. He saw with sure insight into its essential nature. He gave a definition of the Church which holds as well for our time as his own. It lays hold of what is common to a true church, whenever and wherever it is formed. Paul's thought is that a genuine church is *"the body of Christ."* See Ephesians 4:12; Romans 12:4, 5; I Corinthians 12:12-26; Colossians 1:18, and 3:14-15. That is, a church is a *social organism in which Christ's spirit prevails.* The word "body," or organism, is a very suggestive figure of speech. Note several characteristics of a body which apply to a church.

A Body Is a Living Unity-in-Diversity. A stump is a unity, a solitary chunk of wood. A brush pile is a diversity, a collection or aggregate of parts of a tree. A living tree is a unity-in-diversity. It has one life moving through all its parts. What would a tree be that had no parts, a tree without limbs, roots, bark, sap, or leaves? It would be a nonentity. On the other hand, if you should tie the parts together, limbs to trunk, twigs to limbs, and leaves to twigs you would have, not a tree, but an aggregate of dead pieces. A living tree has an inner unity which binds the parts together. The parts exist for the whole; the whole is the life of the parts.

Now a genuine church manifests this vital interrelationship of whole and parts. A real church has a *unity of spirit,* the spirit which was in Christ. It has a common faith in its Lord. It shares a common hope that through the grace of God all things will eventually work together for good. Its members possess a common love for one another and a common concern for the good of the whole group. A divided church is a contradiction in terms. There should be in a church the mystic sense of oneness that prevails in a fraternity, though of a distinctly religious quality.

A rightly ordered church is characterized also by *diversity*. It has variety of membership. It has many individuals in its ranks, no two alike. A church encompasses *natural and social differences*. "By one spirit," says Paul to the Corinthians, "are we all baptized into one body, whether we be Jews or Greeks, slaves or free" (I Cor. 12:13). The Church is broader than the racial distinctions between Jew and Gentile; it bridges the gulf between slave and freeman which law and custom had established.

A true church includes *various psychological types*. In another passage Paul says to the Corinthians, "Give no offense to Jews or to Greeks or to the church of God, . . ." (I Cor. 10:32). The "Jews" were the morally minded, having the most stringent ethical code in antiquity. The "Greeks" represented the cultured world; its capital, Athens, was the symbol of both Reason and Beauty. The "church of God" stood for the devout, the religious-minded people of the community irrespective of their psychological bent. There is a place in the church for all of these.

A genuine church includes *diversities of gifts*. One- two- and five-talented persons will be at home in it. A first-rate church requires a diversity of functions: teaching, evangelism, music, money-raising, and the menial tasks of keeping the building comfortably warm and clean. A church, we reiterate, like the living organism, possesses both unity and diversity. A religious regiment, where every one is expected to keep step and obey unquestioningly a superior who gives the orders, is not a church. On the other hand, a company of people who happen to sit in the same sanctuary on Sunday morning, only to disperse afterward like a movie crowd, is not a church either. A really vital Christian community occurs when people outwardly diverse are united in a common spirit of loyalty to Christ and of love for one another.

A CHURCH IS A FELLOWSHIP. The Greek word which Paul uses for "church" is *koinonia*. It was originally a commercial term which implied co-partnership. Thus, in the Gospels the sons of Zebedee and of John are said to have been *koinonoi*—joint partners in a fishing enterprise. This term the Christians carried over into their church life. They were sharers, co-partners, in a religious enterprise. They shared a great memory of Jesus Christ their Lord. They shared a common experience of God's forgiveness and power. They shared a common hope that Jesus would return and establish his kingdom. They shared in the services of worship, of prayer, and in the breaking of bread. For a while they even shared their material goods. They were comrades in a glorious venture. They regarded themselves as belonging to a common family, "the household of faith." They called each other "brethren." They greeted one another at their meetings with a kiss, after the fashion of Eastern lands. Their sacrament, the Lord's Supper, was a meal, linked to a dinner table, the central social institution in the home. The early church was a far-flung brotherhood of men and women, joined together in the bonds of Christian love, who could be counted on to give meat to the hungry and drink to those who were athirst, to take in the stranger, clothe the naked, and visit those in sickness and in prison. Modern lodges are pale replicas of the spirit of fraternity that breathed through the first Christian communities.

Is there any greater need in the church today than the need for fellowship? We are so rich in money, ideas, equipment, and members, and so poor in love. "Many city churches," as Dr. Charles E. Jefferson once observed, "are made up of people who do not even know one another, and who do not want to know one another. Too many village churches are composed of people who know one another, and are sorry that they do." [1]

It is well to remind ourselves that before the Church had organization, buildings, or liturgy, it was *a fellowship*. And whenever the Church has been true to its genius, it has remained a fellowship. A church is not primarily a building; in some of the most glorious days of its history, like its Lord, it had no home to call its own. A church is more than a congregation. An audience of people, sitting in one place like bottles in the rain, *passively receiving* the gifts of heaven but *not communicating*—that is a travesty on a church. A church is not a hierarchy of officials, important though they may be. A church is a fellowship, named after Him who once said, "I have called you friends." "By this all men will know that you are my disciples, if you have love for one another" (John 15:15; 13:35).

A BODY IS A SERVANT TO THE SPIRIT. How handicapped even the most potent personality is when its body is sick or paralyzed! The natural arrangement is body and spirit in living interaction; the body as a means to the purposes envisaged by the spirit; the body, not an end in itself, but ruled by the spirit. So the true Church is the servant of Christ, its sovereign spirit. The Christian impulse cannot make its way in the world unless it takes a worldly form. The Church is that embodiment. A church which is not ruled by Christ's spirit is dead. A church is the place where the spirit of Christ resides. When he was here, his body was the location where his spirit was at home. Now the Church, where two or three are gathered together, domiciles

34

[1] Charles E. Jefferson, *The Building of the Church* (New York: The Macmillan Company, 1911), p. 52. Used by permission.

his spirit. The Church is the place where his spirit is best revealed. Men never saw Christ's spirit when he was here, —no man, with his eyes, has seen spirit at any time. But in the bearing and movements of his body, in the expression of his face, in the deeds of his hands, his spirit was revealed. Thus today the spirit of Christ makes itself evident mainly in the words, attitudes, and deeds of his Church which is the main instrument by which Christ works in the world.

"When Jesus moved along the lanes of Galilee and the streets of Jerusalem the eyes of his body sought out human need, his ears heard and reported the cry for help, his feet bore him upon errands of mercy, and his hand reached out to life, to heal and bless." [1] Similarly the Church is his eyes, his ears, his lips, his hands in the vast enterprise of redeeming needy humanity.

As a Body Requires a Skeleton if it is to stand erect and to move effectively toward its purpose, so a church must have an organizational structure. As we have already seen, the primitive Church had next to no organization. Its first concern was with the fellowship and the imminent return of the Lord. But as the days lengthened into history and inner hopes were translated into outer facts, the Church was forced to develop an organization. Leadership and authority had to be established and provision had to be made for succession. The faith required interpretation and formulation so as to exclude error from teaching and evangelizing.

Very soon (early enough to be included in the New Testament), provision had to be made for the collection and expenditure of funds (Acts 11:29-30). A little later

[1] C. R. Brown, *The Honor of the Church* (Boston: Pilgrim Press, 1922), p. 41.

properties had to be held and managed. Worship could not continue long without standards enforceable on those who would not keep the peace. Thus, whether the early Church wanted to or not, it found itself acquiring the muscles and sinews of organization.

We have some very "spiritual" persons who insist that they are religious but who do not believe in institutions like the Church—which makes about as much sense as to say that one believes in health but not in hospitals, in education but not in schools, in love but not in homes. Every human interest requires an organization to serve it.

A BODY (and likewise a church) Is A WHOLE OF INTER-DEPENDENT PARTS. The organs are different in function, but each makes its own contribution. Each supplies a capacity which the others lack. The whole is weakened if any organ is lost or fails to function, for none can adequately take the place of any other. To use Paul's own illustration, if the whole body were an eye, how would it hear? If the body were one great ear, where would be the sense of smell? See I Corinthians 12:17. The eye must not say to the hand, I have no need of you, nor the head to the feet, I have no need of you (I Cor. 12:14-20). Each has its own indispensable function without which the others are handicapped.

The application to a church is obvious. Each participating member should honor all the others. The man of means who can give but not teach should not think because he pays the greater share of the bills that he is more important than the worker in the Sunday school. The person who gives of his mind should not look down on the person who does the footwork of the church kitchen. Each person's contribution is different but essential.

A Body Is So Put Together That What Hurts One Organ Hurts All (I Cor. 12:26). Plato observes in his *Republic* that we do not say, " 'My finger is in pain' " but " '*I* have a pain in my finger.' " The whole body suffers when one of its members is injured. When one's digestion is out of order, he is ill all over. An infected foot may cause a fever to rise in the head. We are, to use Paul's famous phrase, "members one of another" (Rom 12:5).

So in a church what hurts one member hurts the others. It is as foolish for church members to quarrel as it is for the right arm to smite the left. It is impossible to wound one's fellow-Christians without doing injury to one's own best interests. Conversely, when one honors his brother he exalts himself eventually. What a revolution would take place in our thought and action if we caught this insight of Paul's that we belong to one organism in Christ!

To go a step further, the parts of the body are so intimately joined together that one dies if it be severed from the whole. Cut off a hand from the body and it ceases to be a hand and becomes a putrescent object. Similarly, a person cannot be a Christian long apart from the Church. Protestants have sometimes been prone to ridicule the Roman Catholic dogma which holds that there is no salvation outside the Church. Of course, there is salvation outside the Roman Church, but there is no salvation outside the Church Universal, the Christian tradition in the large. The Church in the broad sense is the link between Christ and the individual believer.

THERE COME TIMES WHEN THE BODY MUST SACRIFICE ONE OF ITS ORGANS for the health of the whole. If a hand "offends," it may be necessary to cut it off to save the life of the body. Likewise, operations are at times necessary in a church. Members who infect others with false doctrines or ill will, or who are generally uncooperative, must occasionally be gently but firmly removed from the body of the church for the church's own health. More than once a church has actually grown by subtraction of those who were destroying its peace and welfare.

AGAIN, A BODY IS A UNION OF CHANGE AND IDENTITY. Physiologists tell us that the contents of the body cells are completely renewed every seven years. We do not have a cell in our body identical with one of those we had seven years ago. One wit has observed that no husband ever celebrates his tenth wedding anniversary with the woman he married! They both have been completely renewed! Yet, one of the mysteries of life is that despite this continuing physical change, we recognize ourselves as the same persons we have always been. A man of seventy has outgrown ten bodies yet he knows himself to be identical with all his former selves.

So a church is a constantly changing entity. Its personnel changes; pillars of the church pass on and others replace them. Ministers come and go. Beliefs are modified with the years. Organizations adjust themselves to new conditions. It is folly to think one can prevent this process of change. It is even more nonsensical to believe that the process of change can be reversed and that a church can turn back to its past. This would be tantamount to asserting that a man of fifty could become a boy of five. The Church matures as men and women do; since Paul's day we have learned valuable truths under God's tutelage. So long as we perceive our continuity, so long as we serve the Lord in new ways, by new kinds of organization, with different personnel, so long as we remain one in spirit with the past—just so long are we entitled to the honored name of "Christian."

A BODY LIVES BY APPROPRIATING WHAT IS NOT ITSELF AND TRANSFORMING IT INTO ITS OWN NATURE. A living thing cannot exist long off itself. When Christ was here his body received and assimilated the food offered him in Judea and Galilee and transformed it into the energy which spoke and loved and lived in his benign presence.

Similarly, the Church, as Christ's body, must literally live off its world. It must reach out and lay hold of the unredeemed and transform them by divine grace into Christians. The Church is Christ's continued incarnation in the world, making over humanity into his [Christ's] own likeness. This means that *the Church must evangelize, or it starves the body of Christ*. It must not only add names to its roster but must also assimilate people into its life. This is the condition of its survival.

As I write I have the report of our Board of Evangelism before me: 1,911 charges in the Methodist Church received not a soul into their membership on profession of faith in the preceding year. If that record continues the prognosis is death!

A BODY HAS AN AMAZING POWER OF SELF-MAINTENANCE. One basic difference between an organism and a machine is that the organism knows how to minister to its own needs. When the body is weary it refreshes itself with

39

sleep. If it falls ill, the white defenders in the blood repel the invading disease. Whether a person walks beneath the sun or luxuriates in the cool shade, the marvelous thermostatic control of the body keeps his temperature constant.

So a living church has a power of self-maintenance that defies worldly calculation. The Church keeps going through lean years and fat. It operates in democratic lands but also under repressions and behind iron curtains. It purges itself of infections by discipline when alien influences get into its blood stream. Sometimes it is cursed with conflict and division, yet by skillful pastoral work it salves its own wounds. Often it has gone into a coma that the superficial observer took for death, only to come back renewed and strengthened. The Church is the oldest living institution in every community, a fact made possible by its marvelous power of self-repair.

FINALLY, LIFE COMES ONLY FROM LIFE. Bodies cannot be produced artificially. Even if all the chemical ingredients which go to make up an organism could be combined in the proper proportions to produce a synthetic being, the spark of life would be missing. If a species fails to reproduce itself it dies, and no scientific sleight of hand can create another.

Likewise, the modern Church is the scion of a long tradition of religious life. If that tradition were ever lost, Christianity would become extinct. If, for example, all the books of mathematics in the world were to be destroyed, men, by reflecting on the nature of physical quantities, could deduce geometry again, spinning it out of their own minds. But if, perchance, the memory of Christ were completely expunged from human consciousness, his life-story would be lost forever. No one could ever re-create it. How important, therefore, that the Christian tradition be kept intact!

The attempts perennially made to abolish Christianity and the Church and to start over again are foredoomed to failure. A new religion can no more be produced synthetically than a living person can be. When the flame of faith burns low the answer is to get back to the source of the Christian life, Jesus Christ. For only through the touch of life can we have life.

Thus, for Paul, the Church is an organism: a fellowship, an organization, a commonweal, a growth, a redemptive agency, a self-maintaining mechanism, a continuing tradition. How much is suggested by the Apostle's dictum that the Church is "the body of Christ"!

Paul, of course, is painting the ideal! This is the actual Church only in its best hours. Paul's "Church" is a good bit like a loyal alumnus' "Alma Mater," or a patriot's "American way of life," an idealization, a dream of her meaning. Paul was under no illusion as to the actual churches of flesh and bone to which he wrote in Ephesus, Thessalonica, and Rome. Yet he saw with sure eyes what Christ intended them to be and what with God's help they could become. Human though the Church may appear as the alien observer looks upon her in her origin, in her best moments, and in her destiny, she is divine. To remember this is the greatest spur to realizing this ideal, until at last —to employ Paul's own words—she stands before her Lord, the "glorious church, not having spot, or wrinkle, or any such thing; but . . . holy and without blemish" (Eph. 5:27; A.V.).

III

THE MISSION OF
THE CHURCH

Ephesians
+
Colossians

III

What, now, is the purpose of that social organism called the Church, whose characteristics we sketched in Chapter II? In a sentence, *the mission of the Church is to reconcile the world unto God through Christ.* This conception of the Church's task is set forth in two famous letters, the Epistle to the Ephesians, and the Epistle to the Colossians. We shall be concerned with them in this chapter.

THE LETTER TO THE EPHESIANS

This notable letter is, in a sense, a misnomer. The Epistle to the "Ephesians" was not addressed to the church at Ephesus alone, but was actually a circular letter to the groups of saints and faithful Christians of all the Roman provinces of Asia Minor, of which the Ephesian Church was one. The reasons which have led scholars to this conclusion are: (1) To begin with, in Ephesians there is an almost complete absence of the allusions and personal greetings with which Paul was accustomed to adorn his writings. (In some letters, such as Romans, Colossians, and Philemon, half a chapter or more is devoted to proper names of people to whom Paul wished to be remembered.) (2) The local problems of administration and discipline, which must have existed in Ephesus, are not even mentioned. This is especially noteworthy, because the Apostle had labored at Ephesus for at least three years, and had made it his base of operations for the whole of Asia. See Acts 19:10, 26; 20:31. Indeed Paul talks as though he were known to his readers only by hearsay, as one of the "holy apostles" (Eph. 3:1, 2, and 5), and that he had second-hand knowledge of them; "I also, after I heard of your faith in the Lord Jesus, and love toward all the saints" (Eph. 1:15, A.V.). The non-Ephesian character of the letter confirms itself, further, by the fact that the earliest manuscripts do not mention Ephesus in their address, but simply read: "Paul, an apostle of Christ Jesus by the will of God, to the saints who are also faithful in Christ Jesus" (cf. Eph. 1:1 in R.S.V. and A.V.).

This general nature of the letter has led some scholars to question whether the Apostle wrote it at all, especially when experts in Greek report that the vocabulary and style differ greatly from those found in letters of unquestioned Pauline authorship. But such a rejection runs squarely into the fact that the early Fathers of the Church frequently quote from the letter, and they never question its genuineness. As suggested above, they do not connect it with Ephesus, but they always associate it with the Apostle. Several imitations of Paul have come down to us, but they are so obviously feeble and second-rate that few have been fooled by them.

If this letter did not come from Paul's pen it is surely Pauline in substance. There is nothing in Ephesians which Paul might not have written. The style is distinctive and different, yet reminiscent of his other writings. The leading ideas are anticipated elsewhere, though some of them are presented here in a more advanced form. If another brain and hand actually composed this letter, we may be sure that the author was a close disciple of Paul, of great gifts, deeply dyed in the thought of the Apostle, closely acquainted with his letters, and one who spoke in his own way the message which Paul himself would have given. We may say that Paul communicates his message to us as truly in Ephesians as Christ speaks to us in the Gospels, which, although inspired by him, were not literally penned by our Lord himself.

As we have already hinted, the Epistle to the Ephesians is addressed to the whole Christian world. It sees the Christian movement not as an association of local congregations but as a world society and speaks to it in its corporate capacity. The theme of Ephesians is church unity in the framework of world unity.

THE MESSAGE OF EPHESIANS: CHURCH UNITY IN WORLD UNITY

THE DISCORD OF THE WORLD. The message of Ephesians boils down to three fundamental ideas: First, *the world as we now see it is the scene of endless discord.*

47

1. To begin with, *there is the cosmic conflict between good and evil spirits.* "For we are not contending against flesh and blood, but against the principalities, against the powers, against the world rulers of this present darkness, against the spiritual hosts of wickedness in the heavenly places" (Eph. 6:12). As some of our contemporaries claim that the air is alive with flying saucers and unseen visitors from outer space, so the men of Paul's time thought that our world was peopled with invisible spirits. They were of two kinds: God and his angels; Satan and his demons. They were in constant warfare with one another, and the fate of mankind rested upon the outcome of this struggle. The battles of virtue against vice are but pale replicas of a struggle going on in the supernatural sphere. Paul sums up the forces pitted against God in the terms, "principalities" and "powers" (devils), "the world rulers of the present darkness" (the pagan gods of antiquity—Zeus, Isis, Mythras, Serapis, and the like), and "spiritual hosts of wickedness in heavenly places" (the evil stars of astrology).

While few men today would describe evil in the "spirit" terms of the first century, anyone who has ever tackled wickedness has felt that he, like Paul, was fighting not merely flesh and blood, but a foe truly superhuman in its malignant perverseness.

2. Then there is the conflict not only between God and the demon world but *between Him and rebellious men.* Ephesians 2:2 refers to "the sons of disobedience." These are the children of men who insist on living their own lives, who resent the claims of God to control them. They are

the prodigal sons and daughters who prize living in the far country of their own choosing above enjoying the blessings of a Father's governance. They prefer evil (so long as it is their own) to righteousness that implies allegiance to One above self.

Their end is sin, of which Ephesians 4:17-19 is a classic census: They are characterized by "futility of their minds;" they do not believe that life has meaning or direction. They are "darkened in their understanding" because of their unbelief. As the Master put it in the Sermon on the Mount, "If then the light that is in you is darkness, how great is the darkness!" See Matthew 6:23. They are, of course, "alienated from the life of God." They are guilty of "ignorance" and "hardness of heart"; they deliberately steel themselves against every good impulse until they are at last beyond feeling—"callous." Many have given themselves up to "licentiousness," and "every kind of uncleanness," *i.e.,* sexual perversion.

How peculiar that men persist in thinking of freedom in negative terms, as liberty *from* restraint, and thereby missing the values of positive freedom, freedom *for* exalted living!

3. But there is not only discord in the secular world, there is *disunion within the Church.* He admonished the Ephesians, "No longer be children, tossed to and fro and carried about with every wind of doctrine, by the cunning of men, by their craftiness in deceitful wiles" (Eph. 4:14). There were changing fashions of belief in the Church that were unsettling the faithful. Heretics were abroad. Sects and party cries were prevalent.

In addition, there were rivalries among the various officers in the Church. There is good evidence that Paul's statement of the blessings of divers offices and gifts in the Church (Eph. 4:11-12) was medicine for church cleavages. Whatever the situation in Ephesus and the churches thereabouts, at Corinth—as we shall see in Chapter V—the quarrel over offices and gifts split the Church wide open. Office seeking has sunk many modern churches.

4. There was *domestic tension,* even in Christian homes. Read Ephesians 5:21 through 6:9. An old teacher of mine used to say that men and women talk most about the wonders of love when they are falling out of it! When the real thing exists, its own presence is sufficient witness. "Wives," says the author of Ephesians, "be subject to your husbands." "Husbands, love your wives." Why should he admonish them if there were not households—sufficient in number to demand notice—where husband and wife were out of tune? "Children, obey your parents . . . 'Honor your father and mother.'" "Fathers, do not provoke your children to anger" (Eph. 6:1-4). That is, avoid harshness or unfairness, discipline dictated by selfish adult whims, nagging, bullying methods that evoke resentment in the child. Pearl Buck in her book of reminiscences, *My Several Worlds,* reports that as a child she roundly disliked her stern Presbyterian missionary father, even to the point of saying in his hearing that she hated him.[1] Sometimes enmity makes its nest in orthodox Christian households. "Slaves [house servants], be obedient to those who are your earthly masters," "Masters, . . . forbear threatening" (Eph. 6:5, 9).

Our purpose in citing these passages is not to commend

[1] She later outgrew this attitude and came to appreciate her father (p. 99).

their morality. Paul and the men of his time took male dominance for granted. Socially, the Apostle was a conservative and did not question the prevailing institution of slavery. These admonitions are offered because they afford us, as it were, flashlight pictures of the domestic life of early Christians. Though they worshiped a God of love and sang the praises of Christian brotherhood, they had quite as much difficulty in making affection the rule of their homes as we do in our generation.

5. *Personality conflicts.* "We all once lived in the passions of our flesh, following the desires of body and mind, and so we were by nature children of wrath, like the rest of mankind" (Eph. 2:3). The plural of the terms "passions" and "desires" which the author employs, suggests the disintegrated type of individual—familiar to every student of human nature. People of this kind live by irrational impulse, by the compass of ever-fluctuating impulses, never the same two days in succession. They lack a single governing purpose. They are not drawn from before and above by a transcendent principle, but are pulled from behind and below by the beast, the ape and the tiger—the animal in man's make-up.[1] These are the people in whose souls a civil war is going on. They are unhappy, frustrated, ineffective, and truly lost. Ephesians rightly calls them "children of wrath." They know no peace here and can anticipate none in a life to come.

This description of conditions prevailing in the first century is just as accurate a portrait of our time. The late Doctor Henry Sloane Coffin wrote that if there is one word that characterizes our present world it is the word,

[1] Alfred Lord Tennyson, *"In Memoriam,"* CXVIII, Stanza 7.

"split." The world is split vertically into nations, who snarl at one another like scavengers over bones, no man knowing the day nor the hour when atomic war may break out. These belligerent nations are split horizontally into races. In some lands the venom aroused by differing tints of skin exceeds in bitterness the hatred of the enemy beyond the boundary. Not only are the nations sundered horizontally into races, but races are split obliquely into classes. Civil war between labor and management is a constant phenomenon, and the strife between the "haves" and the "have-nots" shows no ceasing. Not only are races split obliquely into classes; within classes there are divided homes. Our record currently is one divorce for every three marriages, and who can compute the amount of domestic misery that never comes to court? Finally, within these broken homes are split personalities. In World War II the Army turned down one person out of every eight as a psychoneurotic. Our globe today is a seething caldron of dissension. The starting point of Ephesians is actually our contemporary condition.

GOD'S RECONCILING PURPOSE. Now it is God's great purpose to overcome the discord in his world by *reconciling, or uniting, all things to himself in Jesus Christ*. The golden verses of Ephesians are 1:9-10: "For he has made known to us in all wisdom and insight the mystery of his will, according to his purpose which he set forth in Christ as a plan for the fullness of time, to unite all things in him, things in heaven and things in earth." For the Apostle, God's grand design for His universe is to bring everything into harmony. This "plan" was in the divine mind when

He created the earth. For eons of time it remained a "mystery"—a secret known to God alone. Then he revealed it to his creation in Jesus Christ. His purpose is to still the jangling discords of the world and to bring all "things in heaven and things in earth" into tune, so that the marvelous order which obtains among the orbits of the stars may prevail among his human creatures.

Because hostility to God is the root of all other discord, his ultimate purpose is to reconcile to himself all those who are at odds with him—the conscious rebels, who like the Prodigal, mutiny against their Father's love, rejoicing in their ungodliness; the semi-conscious aliens, like the wandering sheep, aware that they are lost but ignorant of their way home; the unconscious strangers to God's love, symbolized by the lost coin, not even aware of spiritual need, and hence without the promptings to penitence. His purpose is to weld all humanity into a single brotherhood so that "nation shall not lift up sword against nation" (Isa. 2:4), that races may dwell in mutual respect, class antagonisms dissolve, disharmony within the Church yield to brotherhood, and the bickering tensions in the home be replaced by tender affection.

God's purpose is to bring harmony into human nature, to knit into Christ-dominated unities the unraveled personalities of the mentally and morally sick. God's goal is to gather all the present warring forces of the world "into the unity of the faith and of the knowledge of the Son of God" (Eph. 4:13).

The proof that this is God's aim lies in what has been happening. Read Ephesians 2:4-21. He has saved individuals: "But God, who is rich in mercy, out of the great love with which he loved us, even when we were dead through our trespasses, made us alive together with Christ" (2:4, 5). He has already dissolved the enmity of Jew and Gentile: "Remember that you [the Gentiles] were at that time separated from Christ, alienated from the commonwealth of Israel, . . . But now in Christ Jesus you who once were far off have been brought near in the blood of Christ . . . who has made us both one, and has broken down the dividing wall of hostility" (2:12-14). What God has already wrought is prophetic of the universal concord to come.

If Paul were writing in our time he would see God's purpose confirmed by world affairs. For anyone who peers beneath the surface tensions is aware that the dominant forces of our generation are moving toward unity. *Geographically,* we are rapidly becoming one world. The airplane has made the globe one neighborhood. *Science* does not recognize man-made distinctions: radio impulses do not take out a visa before they cross a boundary line. Even such hideous implements of destruction as the hydrogen bomb witness that men share now in a common fate. No man liveth or dieth to himself any more. *Art* is above parochialism: Who cares, when the Ninth Symphony is performed, what Beethoven's nationality was? The driving forces of *economics* are marching everywhere toward centralization. *Politics,* the most laggard of human interests, cannot avoid the press toward internationalism. We have witnessed a United Nations organization in our generation. *Religion* is keeping step with the progress of men's other concerns; within the last decade a World Council of Churches has been born. While, of course, we are millennia away from the harmony which Ephesians envisages, anyone alive to the trends of the times knows that religion is moving unmistakably toward unity.

THE CHURCH AS THE INSTRUMENT OF RECONCILIATION. The third basic idea of Ephesians is that *the Church is to be God's instrument for effecting the reconciliation of the world.* "That through the church the manifold wisdom of God might now be made known to the principalities and powers" (Eph. 3:10), the beings on the farthest planet will know that God's plan is "that they may all be one" (John 17:21). How magnificently the Apostle conceives the destiny of the Church! It is not just a little company of worshipers, burrowing in the catacombs in cowering fear of the powers of the earth. It is a cosmic force itself, like the sun in the heavens, planted by the Almighty at the center of things to remind his creation of their unity in Christ.

The letter conceives this reconciling status of the Church under three figures of speech: (1) The Church is a state: "You are fellow-citizens with the saints" (Eph. 2:19). It is the commonwealth of God's people, which administers, legislates, and watches over the divine ordinances. (2) The Church is a family: "You are . . . members of the household of God" (2:19). It is the place where brotherhood dwells, tender personal relations prevail, and the first lessons of wholesome cooperation are taught. (3) The

55

Church is a sanctuary: "In whom the whole structure is joined together and grows into a holy temple in the Lord" (Eph. 2:21). It is the place where men worship the One whose unity makes all things one.

What other enterprise besides the Christian Church can hold the world together? Can military power achieve it? It never has. Conquerors have come and gone. The more nearly they have attained perfect unity the shorter their reigns, because the suppression by which they gained their ends evoked the reaction which unseated them.

Will business be able to make the world one? Certainly trade does much to internationalize. As Cordell Hull once affirmed, if nations cannot send goods across their boundaries they eventually send soldiers. But while trade naturally binds the world together, often the traders divide it. For commercial rivalries are among the commonest causes of war.

Will science unify the world? As we have said above, the universalism of science is a powerful force in making the world a neighborhood, but science is ethically neutral and cannot make it a brotherhood. Indeed, science can be employed as easily to separate people as to unite them. The radio can sow the seeds of dissension between the nations whose boundaries it overleaps. The airplane can evoke fear and inspire hatred as well as bring men together.

Can any other religion unify the world? It is doubtful, because few religions are universal in their own nature. No religion which represents only a fragment of humanity can play physician to the divisions of the human spirit and make it one.

If, now, the Church is to be God's agent of unity, three conditions are essential. First, the Church itself must be a unity. Read Ephesians 4:1-16. How can the church preach world unity to the statesmen, economic peace to labor and management, or friendship across the color line, if church-men themselves cannot get together? Their own divisions will speak so loudly that the men of this world will not hear what they have to say about unity. Furthermore, to employ Bishop Brent's memorable phrase, "The world is too strong for a divided church." The enemy is here in full force, and we shall need every ally in order to win. In the face of our task, it is as tragic for us to have interdenominational squabbles as it would be for regiments of the same army to fire on one another.

The Apostle has given us the sevenfold platform of church unity in another golden verse: "There is one body and one Spirit, just as you were called to the one hope that belongs to your call, one Lord, one faith, one baptism, one God and Father of us all who is above all and through all and in all" (Eph. 4:4-6).

"ONE BODY"—that is, one visible organization. I do not believe the Church will convince the world of its unity until men *see* it. Granted that we shall probably have to begin by interdenominational work and worship, eventually there will be some form of organic unity. As Bishop McConnell used to say, "even a company of saints in heaven would need traffic officers!" No matter how greatly the individual

57

constituents of the Church grow in grace, they will not reach maximum effectiveness till there is central direction.

ONE SPIRIT. Organizational unity waits upon a unity of spirit. I passed a church building the other day with the sign above its door, "The Original Church of God." Can we ever have church unity if one denomination believes that it has a corner on validity, or truth, or piety, or polity? We shall become one when we feel that the things we have in common are more fundamental than the points on which we differ.

ONE HOPE. Unity of spirit is furthered as men press on toward common ends. The Church must look forward to one Kingdom, greater than any single denomination, which reaches into the eternal world. Professor William Warren Sweet, in his *Story of Religion in America,* recalls the occasion when George Whitefield, preaching from the courthouse balcony in Philadelphia, cried out:

> " 'Father Abraham, whom have you in Heaven? Any Episcopalians?' 'No.' 'Any Presbyterians?' 'No.' 'Have you any Independents or Seceders?' 'No.' 'Have you any Methodists?' 'No, no, no!' 'Whom have you there?' 'We don't know those names here. All who are here are Christians—believers in Christ—men who have overcome by the blood of the Lamb and the word of his testimony.' 'Oh, is this the case? Then God help us, God help us all, to forget party names, and to become Christians in deed and in truth.' " [1]

ONE LORD. It goes without saying that Christian unity is impossible without Christ. And how can we profess Christ,

[1] William Warren Sweet, *Story of Religion in America* (New York: Harper & Brothers, Revised Edition, 1939), pp. 205-206.

who prayed that his disciples might be one, without having church unity?

ONE FAITH: Unity in conduct presupposes a unity of belief, a common creed. This does not mean that we shall adopt the articles of faith of any single denomination, or that we shall attempt to find the common denominator of all. Rather, we shall seek a totality of those convictions which, devout believers have discovered, make life meaningful. Harry Emerson Fosdick inviting newcomers to Riverside Church used to say, "There are in this church members of many denominations and many faiths. In welcoming you into our membership, we do not ask you to give up any belief or form that is dear to you but rather to bring it in to us that we may be enriched thereby."[1] This is true ecumenicity.

ONE BAPTISM. This does not mean, as one sect contends, that we must all be immersed. It signifies that all genuine Christians will be actually incorporated into the body of Christ, and that baptism is the symbol of this act of incorporation.

ONE GOD. Our connection with God is the one essential relation which, if right, inevitably sets our other relationships right. If we establish communion with the one Father we can never be foes of one another.

Paul's message that the Church is one is the common teaching of the New Testament. The Christian Church did not begin with a multitude of local congregations which finally linked with others to form a universal Church. The Church did not begin with many and finally become one. Rather, it began as one and became many. The Church is

[1] Used by permission.

not a sand heap compounded of thousands of particulars; it is a body, which began as a seed that multiplied indefinitely. The Church began with a little company of Jesus' disciples in Jerusalem who thought of themselves as a family. As they scattered over the Empire they carried their brotherhood of faith with them. The first Christians did not think of themselves as members of the church at Ephesus, or at Corinth, or at Rome. They belonged to the Church, the one universal Church of God, of which the local church was just a branch or manifestation.

Paul would have thought it a scandal to speak of a Methodist or a Baptist Church. He would not have understood a "white" church or a "colored" church. A "white" church is a contradiction in terms, like "wooden iron" or "a round square." By its very nature the Church includes all races. Paul would never have spoken of an "English" or an "American" Church. He believed that Christ came to break down the partition between nationalities (Eph. 1:10).

Since the Church of God unites all men in a common brotherhood, it follows that Christianity is a religion that can lay claim to universality. When once you begin to love men, in Christ's meaning of the term, it is like a light, brightest and warmest to those nearest it, but extending its rays even to the farthest bounds of the universe. Not only is it available to all humanity, it needs the witness of all humanity to bring out its rich content. Some of us remember hearing Professor Halford Luccock describe a line which he had come across in a country newspaper: "Last night at the P.T.A. Mabel Jones whistled the *Fifth Sym-*

phony." Dr Luccock's comment [1] was that while probably Mabel was a nice girl, she couldn't whistle Beethoven's *Fifth*. It takes a symphony to render that. So our religion is too great to be rendered adequately by a single individual, or by Methodists, a single denomination; or by white men, a particular race; or by Americans, a single nation. It requires world Christianity to do it.

One of the great facts of our time is the movement to restore this sense of the Church Universal. Christianity began and for about fifteen centuries essentially remained a world fellowship: although after the Council of Chalcedon, in 451, the Syrian Orthodox and the Coptic Churches broke off; and a major organizational split occurred in 1054 when the Church broke in two with an Eastern communion and a Western communion, a disagreement having arisen between the Bishop of Rome and the Bishop of Constantinople. In the sixteenth century came the Protestant Reformation—and it was necessary—shattering the long-standing unity of the Church, and for more than three hundred and fifty years the Christian forces of the Western world moved toward ever-increasing diversity. In that period the major Protestant denominations were born.

But about the beginning of the present century the tide began to turn, the Christians started to consolidate instead of divide. We saw the world conferences—many of them guided by our own great Methodist layman, John R. Mott —at Edinburgh, Stockholm, Lausanne, Jerusalem, Oxford, Madras, Amsterdam. We have witnessed the formation of international Christian organizations,—the World Student Christian Federation, the International Missionary Council,

[1] Halford E. Luccock, *Communicating the Gospel* (New York: Harper & Bros., 1954), p. 94.

the International Council of Religious Education, the World Alliance of the Y.M.C.A. Branches of several denominations have united, as Methodism did in 1939. The denominations have been steadily drawing nearer to one another. The Federal Council of Churches, and then the National Council of Churches, were born. Now a World Council of Churches is a reality. The great movement of our time, religiously speaking, has been toward world Christianity.

To be sure, not everyone has gone along. There are people in our churches who will still fight the support of any cause beyond their local parish or denominational fence. Crass sectarianism is still a force to be reckoned with. "Why don't you come to our church?" one little boy asked of another. "Because," came the reply, "we belong to different abominations." Just so! We still have denominations among us that approach the status of abominations. Yet, the direction of march has been the other way. "There is no speech nor language" today where the voice of ecumenical Christianity is not heard. Truly, "their line is gone out through all the earth, and their words to the end of the world" (Ps. 19:3-4; A.V.).

CHRISTIANS AS RECONCILERS

Not only must there be corporate unity, if we are to have world unity, but there must be reconciling individual Christians. Father James Keller, head of that splendid organization, The Christophers, contends that less than one per cent of humanity has caused the world's troubles.[1] If another one per cent could be persuaded to work as industriously in the

[1] Father James Keller, *You Can Change the World* (New York: Christopher Books, 1948), p. vii.

opposite direction they could change the world. This was Paul's contention, too. If men and women can be found who will be unifiers, they will reverse the forces which divide.

What qualities are essential in people who will be reconcilers? Ephesians 4:4-6 mentions many, but they may be reduced to four:

A LOVING DISPOSITION. If Christians, to use Dr. Fosdick's famous phrase, are to be a part of the answer instead of the problem,[1] they must be "eager to maintain the unity of the Spirit in the bond of peace" (Eph. 4:3). "Let all bitterness and wrath and anger and clamor and slander be put away from you, with all malice, and be kind to one another, tender-hearted, forgiving one another, as God in Christ forgave you. Therefore be imitators of God, as beloved children. And walk in love, as Christ loved us and gave himself up for us" (Eph. 4:31 through 5:2).

The charmed word for Christians and the solution for the world's ills is *love*. What does the New Testament mean by it? Love is *the wholehearted giving of oneself for another's good*. It means giving one's attention, affection, comradeship, and possessions to others that their best may be thereby elicited. Love in the Christian sense differs in three ways from what usually passes for it: First, Christian love is not fundamentally, like romantic love, an emotion but is an act of will. It is not only feeling right toward others but doing right by them. Secondly, Christian love is based on identification of oneself with the other man. When the Master said, "Thou shalt love thy neighbor as thyself," he did not mean "as much as thyself" but *"as*

[1] Harry Emerson Fosdick, *On Being Fit to Live With* (New York: Harper & Bros., 1946), pp. 10-18.

though he were thyself." Christian love is tying one's own sensibilities to the other person's nerve endings, so that one looks at life as he does. In the third place, it is unlimited: It is directed toward all human beings; is not dependent on their returning our love or being good. One must go on forgiving and being kind no matter what the cost to oneself.

Suppose we could set in operation a chain reaction of such sacrificial goodwill. Would it not heal the malignant passions of the times and turn the world toward unity?

TRUTHFUL, EDIFYING SPEECH. "Speaking the truth in love" (Eph. 4:15), to use one of Paul's great phrases, is another quality essential in reconciliation. "Putting away falsehood, let every one speak the truth with his neighbor" (Eph. 4: 25). "Let no evil talk come out of your mouths, but only such as is good for edifying, as fits the occasion, that it may impart grace to those who hear" (Eph. 4:29).

Unification of the world waits on mutual confidence, which in turn rests on truth. But truth-telling alone can be an instrument of division. "The plain, blunt man" who speaks his piece is hardly a promoter of social concord. The speech that makes a better world is that which, while staying within the truth, also builds up. It is loving, productive of others' good.

SELF-RENUNCIATION. "I therefore, a prisoner for the Lord, beg you to lead a life worthy of the calling to which you have been called, with all lowliness and meekness" (Eph. 4:1-2). We shall never call a harmonious society into being by putting on airs, or trying to beat out one another in competition. The spirit of modesty and humility, of egos

64

under restraint, is the key to the united world. I think there is no more winsome picture of "lowliness and meekness" in the life of John Wesley than the occasion of his teaching in a parish school on his visit to Georgia. He found in his classes a number of poor boys laughed to scorn by the young Savannah aristocrats, because they came to their lessons in their bare feet. Sensing the situation, Wesley himself appeared barefoot to catechize the children. Is there any question which attitude—that of Wesley or that of the scoffers —bears the greater promise for a friendly world?

PATIENCE. "Do not let the sun go down on your anger" (Eph. 4:26). The united world will not be achieved by next Thursday. Hostility and wrathful explosions will be the rule for a long while to come. The Christian can further the better day by being patient with men's frailties, quenching the fires that enmity has ignited, and refusing to permit his own hostility to smoulder.

THE MESSAGE OF COLOSSIANS: THE SUPREMACY OF CHRIST

While the Letter to the Ephesians proclaims the unity of the Church, its mission to bring about world unity, and the duty of its members to serve as reconcilers of men, the Letter to the Colossians has a different, though closely related theme, namely, the supremacy of Christ.

The ancient city of Colossae, about one hundred miles east on the highway between Ephesus and the River Euphrates, was the seat of a thriving church. Epaphras, one of Paul's disciples, had founded it. The Apostle himself had never visited the community, but he knew members of the church, and was warmly interested in it. While Paul was imprisoned his friend, Epaphras, brought news that a strange heresy had broken out in the Colossian Church.

Influential persons in the church were denying the supremacy of Christ. The details of their doctrines are not clear from this distance. They seem to have taught that Christ in himself is not sufficient to save. In order to master the material forces of the world men must enlist on their side various angelic beings who prescribed certain ascetic practices and initiation by secret rites into a wisdom superior to the gospel. There was no outright rejection of Christ but a kind of blending of religions.

They taught that there is a gulf between God and the material world too great to bridge, and that between God and creation there is a series of intermediate beings rising tier on tier toward the Divine. Salvation is a process of climbing this spiritual ladder from each being to the one higher. Christ is merely one of the intermediaries, rather than the only begotten Son of God. Under this treatment Christ becomes only half divine rather than "the very God of very God" of the Nicene Creed. Christ is just a rung on the climb up to the Father. Christ is thus demoted from the central role in man's salvation and is made a colleague of Judaic and pagan dignitaries. Epaphras, Paul's friend, was in distress over these philosophic views of his Colossian brothers. So he sought out Paul in prison and laid the situation before him.

The Apostle, shrewdly, did not attack this tendency by attempting to prove the doctrine false. *He accentuated the positive.* He tried to bring home to the Colossians the fact that they already possessed in Christ all the salvation, the perfection, the wisdom that any pagan philosophy could possibly offer. He endeavored to deepen their knowledge (Col. 1:9), to "establish" them in their faith (Col. 2:7), and to arouse their thankfulness for what they already possessed in Christ (Col. 1:12; 2:7; 3:15-17; and 4:2).

CHRIST IS THE COSMIC PRINCIPLE OF UNITY

Paul shows Christ to be supreme in two ways—both crucial for unifying the world. First, Christ is *the cosmic principle of unity* (See Col. 1:15-20). There are some who will ask at once, Why get into theology? metaphysics? Is it not enough to let Christ be our example and to pass up discussions as to the nature of his person?

Furthermore, is Jesus Christ, born of the Virgin Mary and crucified in the first century by Pontius Pilate, of any consequence in this vast universe with its terrifying distances, in which our little earth is but as a millionth part of a grain of sand out of all the sea-sand in the world?

There are those, too, in our day who will raise the questions of the Colossian heretics. Don't we need more than Christ to save the world? Must we not call on the good angels of science, of psychiatry, of politics? Does Christ have anything really significant to offer to our chaotic world?

There is no use trying to bypass these questions. We shall win the best minds of our own generation only by bravely and intelligently facing them. All too often the doors of our churches have been so low that men have been forced to leave their heads outside. A distinguished and beloved religious leader recalls once receiving a whimsical letter from a person saying, "When I go to church I wish I could somehow unscrew my head and put it under the seat with my hat, picking it up on the way out. For in our church you never have use for anything above the collar-button!" Brainless emotionalism will not win our world.

After all, the question as to the nature of ultimate reality is crucial for every one of us, because, in the long run, the universe is going to win. What is the use of trying to fashion a peaceful world if the Creator is himself a Stalin or a Hitler? What hope is there for brotherhood if Nature is heartless, red in tooth and claw? Why be kind and loving if, when life is over, God sacks you and leaves you unremembered on his ash heap of eternal death? What motive can there be for building a meaningful earth if the universe as a whole is meaningless? To think that we can establish a just and loving society in a heartless universe is as foolish as to try to grow oranges inside the Arctic Circle. Is the climate for or against us as we try to raise a crop of kindness on our earth? That is the basic question.

Now what Paul tries to tell us in Colossians is that we can march forward with confidence toward the goal of a harmonious world, because God is like Jesus Christ. The Apostle puts his thought in the philosophy of another day, but that is his meaning. Christ "is the image of the invisible God" (1:15). "In him all things were created, in heaven and on earth, visible and invisible, whether thrones or dominions or principalities or authorities—all things were created through him and for him" (1:16). That is, Christ was in the great Architect's mind as he fashioned his universe: the spirit which we see in the Master is the model of what God planned for his creation. The world was put together Christ-wise. "He is before all things, and in him all things hold together" (Col. 1:17). As the President of the United States is the visible unity of our country, a symbol in the eyes of humanity of what America is like, so Christ is a visible symbol of what Ultimate Reality, or God, is. "For in him all the fullness of God was pleased to dwell" (Col. 1:19). There is nothing in God's nature which is not present in Christ: there is nothing that one will ever learn about God which will contradict what he has seen and heard in Jesus. Christ unveils before our eyes the inner meaning of the world. All this visible creation exists not for its own sake, but in order to reveal the divine purpose manifested in Christ.

Because God is like Christ we are entitled to fight bravely for a warless world, to pacify the antagonisms in industry, to scotch the vipers of race prejudice. We have the assurance that God Almighty is behind us. The universe is on the side of the gospel. The world is not moving on toward chaos; it is moving on to Christ. The dominant forces of the universe will conserve what he embodied; they will destroy ultimately what he opposed.

What courage this should give us! I was in Coventry, England, after World War II. The people of that city never forget how their King visited them immediately after their city was obliterated by bombing to remind them, not only that the rest of the land sympathized with them in their misery, but that the resources of an empire were behind them as they began to rebuild. Similarly, Christ is a visitor to us from the Infinite, reminding us that the universe is behind us as we endeavor to put together the broken pieces of our divided world.

In Paul's thought, of course, *the Cross is vital to the reconciliation of the world*. "For in him all the fullness of God was pleased to dwell, and through him to reconcile to himself all things, whether on earth or in heaven, making peace by the blood of his cross," writes Paul (Col. 1:19-20). All the forces in the universe hostile to man—sin, death, the law, the demonic agencies—hurled themselves at Christ. They achieved his Crucifixion. But he arose victorious. He received in his body every wound that evil could inflict— and came back. Through the Cross all the forces making for chaos in the universe were vanquished. Christ thus brought peace, because his death and resurrection destroyed all the mysterious forces which have caused disunion.

CHRIST IS THE SUPREMELY UNIFYING FORCE IN THE CHURCH

In the second place, Christ is supreme because he is *the source of barrier-destroying unity in the Church*. Christ is not only a symbol of the metaphysical unity of creation, he is a practical unifying force on earth. Indeed, the reason why Paul believed Jesus Christ to be of universal significance was the fact that he saved men from their alienation from God. Paul had experienced it himself. Time was when he had been forlorn and divided, a narrow, frustrated legalist. He met Christ and suddenly found himself—like a man who had been rescued from a foul dungeon and put into the sunlit, open air. He breathed in a vast freedom; his spirit longed to do good, and he found a tireless and efficient power with which to do it. He discovered the peace of God, and with divine harmony had come a love for men which his former self would never have dreamed possible.

When he compared notes with his fellow-Christians—the Church—he found that their experiences checked with his. "And you," he writes to the Colossians, "who once were estranged and hostile in mind, doing evil deeds, he has now reconciled" (Col. 1:21-22). "You have come to fullness of life in him, who is the head of all rule and authority" (Col. 2:10). They had been able to put off the body of flesh —impure thoughts, impulses, and desires (Col. 2:11). Those who had been "dead in trespasses" God had "made alive together with him," forgiving them through Christ (Col. 2:13).

The secret, therefore, of producing unity in the world is to stay close to Christ, the great source of unity. Canon Charles E. Raven, a former chaplain to King George VI, and one of England's most distinguished scholars, once wrote, "To see Christ is to love Him: to love Him is to begin to say, 'He lives in me!' " [1] He learned such sentiments from Paul. "As therefore you received Christ Jesus the Lord, so live in him, rooted and built up in him and established in the faith" (Col. 2:6, 7). "Live in him"—the principle of Christian character is contagion. We not only catch disease and acquire vulgarities of speech and posture by

[1] Charles E. Raven, *Jesus and the Gospel of Love* (New York: Henry Holt & Co., 1931), p. 120.

association. The same law operates positively. If we stay long enough with good men and women their virtues rub off on us. They infect us with their graces. We come unconsciously to look at life through their eyes. Their moral power re-enforces our good intents. "Abide in me and I in you," the Master said to his disciples in the upper room. As the vine lays hold of the universal forces, the soil and the sunshine, the rain and the dew, and then sends the pulsations of its own energy into every branch until it bears fruit, so, if we live in Christ, if we maintain an unbroken and vital sense of fellowship with the great Source of unity, our lives will have reconciling qualities of "compassion, kindness, . . . meekness, and patience" (Col. 3:12), and above all, love, "which binds everything together in perfect harmony" (Col. 3:14). "Let the word of Christ" dwell richly in us (Col. 3:16), let us "in word or deed, do everything in the name of the Lord Jesus, giving thanks to God the Father through him" (Col. 3:17), and eventually "the peace of Christ" will rule in our hearts (Col. 3:15) and become a unity-generating force in our sorely divided earth.

Here, then, in summary, is the mission of the Church: to transform the world, alienated from God and at war in its members, into a divine harmony by first making itself a harmony through union with Christ. The Kingdom is heavenly music—"peace on earth, good will toward men" (Luke 2:14; A.V.), and the Church, attuned to her Lord, is God's instrument for its rendering.

IV

THE MESSAGE OF
THE CHURCH

IV

Admitting that the mission of the Church (as we have seen in Chapter III) is to unify the world, the question arises: How is it to be done? And the answer is: by persuasion. The Church of Christ does not propose to reduce the world to unity by military conquest, as Islam did in the Near East, or by persecution and the use of police power to liquidate opposition, as with the mediaeval Inquisition or current practices in Iron Curtain countries. The true Church does not resort to coercion to unify, whether it be the overt knocking of skulls together or the subtler arts of bribery and propaganda. The weapon of the Church is neither power, nor gold, but *ideas*—ideas so true and appealing that they cause men to act cooperatively in the spirit of Christ. The Letter to the Romans is Paul's sketch of the ideas—or message—which the Church must transmit if it would win its world.

These ideas, as we shall see presently, are theological. Paul did not, primarily, offer men good advice. He did not exhort them, initially, to be righteous. He did not preach problem-sermons or show how his hearers might "win friends and influence people." He did not preach ethics directly. Paul's message was a statement about Ultimate Reality, about God, and his Christ. Once catch a vision of God and his Son, Paul believed, and right living will spring from it. Seek the Divine, first, and His righteousness, then all the other human good things—character, peace of mind, friends, influence, and happiness—will be added. Paul's message, therefore, was a set of theological ideas which, if firmly believed and as resolutely acted upon, would unite the world into a Christian commonwealth.

His approach is right. Theology is crucial, for in the long run a person becomes like the God he worships. The person who worships a cruel god becomes cruel in his conduct. The worship of an impersonal deity results in woeful disregard of the value of the individual. The worship of a nationalist deity produces bigoted patriotism. The allegiance to a tribal God produces a people who become exclusive. G. K. Chesterton, the English author, was right when he said that a landlady should first ask a prospective renter his view of the universe! For ultimately one's theology, one's theory of the world, determines the way he lives.

This theological message of Paul's was addressed to the Christians at Rome, the capital of the Empire. It is significant that Paul does not speak of a Roman Church (Rom. 1:7). Rather, Christianity seems to have taken the form of several separate circles meeting in private homes (Rom. 16:5, 15), instead of a unified organization. We know nothing for sure about the origin of the faith in Rome: the claim that Peter founded Christianity in Rome is unhistorical; the Church had been in existence there long before Paul wrote (Rom. 15:23). Presumably the seed of faith had been planted in the Roman capital by immigrants from the East. Paul had labored long in Antioch, Corinth, and Ephesus, cities in constant intercourse with Italy. At a time when there was a ceaseless coming and going of imperial officials—the movement of troops from place to place along the vast frontier, the ever-moving shuttle of commerce, and the lure of the great city to life in the provinces—it would be strange if Christians had not traveled the road that led to Rome.

We can only guess at the make-up of the Christian community in Rome. Probably it ran the gamut of classes from government officials through professional men and craftsmen to servants and slaves, for Rome, a metropolis, embraced all kinds. We can be quite certain that the Christians were an interracial group. The group was predominantly Gentile, as Paul's direct address in Romans 11, and his broad references in Romans 1:5-7, 13-15, and 15:14-16 indicate. But it must have contained many Jews as well, otherwise we are hard put to it to account for the quantity of material dealing with the Mosaic Law, Romans 3:19-20 and 7:7-24, and with the nature of redemption, Romans 3 through 8, and the very lengthy discussion of the fate of Israel, Romans 9 through 11.

Paul wrote the Letter to the Romans from Corinth, Greece. He had finished a long ministry in Ephesus, and was waiting for delegates from the leading churches to join him and travel to Jerusalem with a collection that had been gathered for the poor. In the three months' interval while the delegates assembled he penned his longest and most elaborate letter.

His motives in writing are transparent. He felt that his work in Asia Minor and Greece was done: "I no longer have any room for work in these regions" (Rom. 15:23). Paul was primarily an evangelist, a founder of churches. He had now established a Christian community in practically every major city. Like our pioneer forebears he felt the call of the West. He sought new frontiers and wider horizons. He writes to the Romans, "I have longed for many years to come to you, I hope to see you in passing as I go to Spain, and to be sped on my journey there by you, once I have enjoyed your company for a little" (Rom. 15:23-24). Christ had already been preached in Italy, and Paul looked forward to Spain as a new field of evangelistic work. On the journey to the West he hoped to tarry a bit at Rome, of which he had often heard. The Letter to the Romans, then, is in anticipation of a visit which the Apostle hoped to make.

"I long to see you," he writes, "that I may impart to you some spiritual gift to strengthen you, that is, that we may be mutually encouraged by each other's faith, both yours and mine" (Rom. 1:11-12). Paul thought there would be a double advantage. He might be able to make a contribution to their life. It seems highly probable that the Roman Church was conservative in temperament and could profit from the warm, enthusiastic spirit of the Apostle. He was hopeful, too, that their faith might also upbuild his own. It is quite likely that the Apostle had in mind even more tangible support than the spiritual. His strategy had always been to establish a base of operations in a large city from which the gospel radiated into the surrounding country. Probably Paul planned to establish such a center at Rome for work in the West. To that end he wanted to win the sympathy, cooperation, and financial support which would insure the undergirding of his mission.

We think of the Apostle now as *Saint* Paul. In his own time, however, he was a highly controversial figure. Jewish reactionaries were abroad. They had caused him trouble in Galatia and Corinth. Probably the whisperers had already relayed the word to Rome that he was a "subversive." Distorted versions of his views were doubtless already common property. His mission would be futile from the outset if his foes were to entrench themselves in the capital and spread false rumors about him in the West as they had done in the East. So the Apostle sought straightforwardly to introduce himself and the gospel which he had been preaching, the only gospel he felt to be adequate to save and unify the world. In the Roman Epistle, therefore, Paul tries to make himself and his teaching clear to a community which had never known him.

This letter straight from Paul's heart is the despair, however, of his interpreters. The human subconscious is not a deep freeze out of which ideas may be lifted at convenience, neatly packaged and labelled. It resembles more the crater of a volcano, a fierce, fiery, laval fusion of emotion and ideas without clear distinction, or definition, or organization. As Paul warms to his theme he pours out his gospel so that even his ablest expositors are tempted to give up. Especially in Romans the Apostle is at his best (in lofty feeling and depth of thought) and at his worst (in his want of consecutive development of his theme)! There are four major ideas in the Letter, and I have simply tried to collate the material around them:

1. The world needs to be saved from sin (Rom. 1:18 through 3:18).

2. The world can be saved by faith alone (Rom. 3:19 through 8:3).

3. Faith admits men to the life of the spirit, the life of peace, hope, and love (Rom. 8:4-33; and 12:1 through 15:13).

4. While the Jews have rejected this faith, it does not represent a final defeat of God's purposes (Rom. 9:1 through 11:36).

THE WORLD'S NEED TO BE SAVED FROM SIN

Read Romans 1:18 through 3:18. The world in which we live is not only divided, as Paul showed us in Ephesians, it is also in the grip of sin: "All men, both Jews and Greeks, are under the power of sin" (Rom. 3:9). Sin's mastery of men expresses itself in many forms:

IDOLATRY. Men "exchanged the glory of the immortal God for images resembling mortal man or birds or animals or reptiles" (1:23).

SEX PERVERSIONS (Rom. 1:26-27).

ANTISOCIAL ATTITUDES. "They were filled with all manner of wickedness, evil, covetousness, malice. Full of envy, murder, strife, deceit, malignity, they are gossips, slanderers, haters of God, insolent, haughty, boastful, inventors of evil, disobedient to parents, foolish, faithless, heartless, ruthless" (Rom. 1:29-31).

SELF-RIGHTEOUSNESS. To the Gentile he says, "But by your hard and impenitent heart you are storing up wrath for yourself on the day of wrath when God's righteous judgment will be revealed" (Rom. 2:5). To the Hebrews: "But if you call yourself a Jew and rely upon the law and boast of your relation to God and know his will and approve what is excellent, because you are instructed in the law, . . . you then who teach others, will you not teach yourself? . . . You who boast in the law, do you dishonor God by breaking the law?" See Romans 2:15-23.

This state of sin means that "the wrath of God" is in store for humanity (Rom. 1:18; 2:4-12). By "wrath of God" Paul does not mean that God gets red-faced and angry, but that there is a day of inexorable judgment upon evil, and "the wages of sin is death" (Rom. 6:23).

Now Paul's idea of sin differs in several ways from our own:

1. We think of sin as a deed; he thought of it as a *condition*. If I steal, I sin. For Paul "sin" is the underlying evil state of affairs of which the stealing is a symptom. When a thermometer registers 104°, the thermometer does not have the fever. It merely records for the world to see that the patient's condition is serious. So the evil acts mentioned in the paragraphs above are evidence of a state of wrongness in human nature and the world.

2. We tend to think of sin impersonally; at least most

modern men have given up the notion of a personal devil. But Paul regards sins as *a demonic power* outside of an individual, which acts upon him, if possible forcing entrance into his life and reducing him to bondage and causing him to transgress. The Apostle uses such phrases as "sin revived" [literally, "sprang to life"] and "I died" (Rom. 7:9); "sin ... deceived me, and ... killed me" (Rom. 7:11); "it is no longer I that do it, but sin which dwells within me" (Rom. 7:17).

3. We are inclined to associate sin with individual men, as, Judas Iscariot was a sinner. Or, a murderer is a sinner. For Paul *sin is a universal fact,* true of each man because it is true of all mankind. "All men are under the power of sin," he contends, quoting from the Psalms: "None is righteous, no, not one; no one understands, no one seeks for God. All have turned aside, together they have gone wrong; no one does good, not even one" (Rom. 3:10-12).

4. We tend to assign various degrees to sin. No one would question that a brutal murder is a sin. But then there are other acts which are, perhaps, only half sinful. We speak of flattering a hostess, for instance, as a "white lie"; it is neither clearly a transgression nor a deed of kindness. It partakes of both. For Paul, however, there is *a sharp dualism* between sin and righteousness. The works of the Devil and the works of God are as different as day and night, and there is no twilight.

5. The seat of sin for Paul is in the flesh. Paul differeniates between three terms: *the body, the flesh,* and *the spirit.* The "body," he holds, is really what we mean by "personality," the total character of an individual. The "flesh"

is the selfish instinct in a human being. It is the side of him that wants [i.e. craves or aspires]. It may take the form of a crudely physical impulse, as the desire of sex or hunger; it may, at a higher level, reveal itself as the urge for favor or power. Whenever a person yields to the "flesh"—his selfish wants—the result is "corruption" or sin, the decay or rotting of personality. The "spirit," on the other hand, is God operative in human nature, and its consequence is "eternal life." As Paul sums it up in Galatians, "For he who sows to his own flesh will from the flesh reap corruption; but he who sows to the Spirit will from the Spirit reap eternal life" (Gal. 6:8).

There has been a tendency in our time to pooh-pooh the idea of sin. Harold Nicolson, one of England's most distinguished biographers, said a while ago, "When I look back upon the more than sixty years that I have spent on this entrancing earth and when I am asked which of all the changes that I have witnessed appears to me to be the most significant, I am inclined to answer that it is the loss of a sense of shame." [1] Several reasons account for this phenomenon. One is the confusion of righteousness with respectability, the assumption that if a person is cultured he is therefore good. There is the equally confusing identification of sin with murder, theft, or adultery, which, conveniently, lets most of us off. Or, we may have deteriorated spiritually so slowly that we are unaware of our condition. We are like some individuals who, approaching retirement, protest that they are just as good—physically—as they ever were, which is *prima facie* evidence that their vision is slipping! For everyone else can perceive the fact they fail

[1] Harold Nicolson, in *Quote* (Indianapolis: Droke House), Mar. 16, 1952, p. 11.

to see, namely, that they are not as strong as they once were.

Now sin, for Paul, is wrongness, the tendency of life to get fouled up. Do you feel that there is anything wrong with yourself or the world? If you do, "sin" is present. If a person is under any doubt about the existence of "sin" there are three questions he may ask: First, is there anything I feel guilty about? Is there anything in my conduct of today or yesterday for which I reproach myself? Do I sometimes wish I could send my life to the cleaners? Then sin is present. Secondly, is there anything for which I blame others? Then certainly sin exists in them, which creates a strong presumption that the same condition exists in me. As Paul puts it, "you have no excuse, O man, whoever you are, when you judge another; for in passing judgment upon him you condemn yourself, because you, the judge, are doing the very same things" (Rom. 2:1). In the third place, am I unhappy? In general, if we live right, we feel right, spiritually as well as physically. If we feel miserable, it is a sure sign that we are violating one of God's laws. A candid look at the world today, and the individuals who make it up, would confirm Paul's judgment that, "all men . . . are under the power of sin" (Rom. 3:9).

SALVATION BY FAITH ALONE
(Romans 3:19 through 8:3)

Now it was the Apostle's deepest conviction that men can never gain deliverance from this mastery of sin through the remedy proposed by the Jewish religion, that is, obedience to the Mosaic Law. For while the Law made men aware of their sinfulness, it did not give them the power to overcome it. The moral law may tell us what we ought to do, but it does not put our feet actually in the way nor give us strength for the journey. Our conscience tells us that we ought not to hate, to cheat, to gossip, to drink, and yet men go on doing these things. Muriel Lester, the distinguished English religious leader, tells about an old gossip who used to come to her meetings. The woman knew she ought to give up taletelling. In her better moments she sincerely wanted to do so. She would often go for weeks without saying a single unkind word, then she would fall —going into a veritable binge of vituperation, and her tongue would cause all manner of heartache and injury— to those she loved and hated, alike—through her talebearing and gossip. She would then come back all penitent. Once she said, "Miss Lester, God Almighty never made a better woman than I, but I just can't live up to it!" [1] She speaks for the race. She speaks for Paul himself as he confesses, in the great seventh chapter of Romans, where he recounts his experiences with the law, "I do not understand my own actions. . . . I can will what is right, but I cannot do it. For I do not do the good I want, but the evil I do not want is what I do. . . . Wretched man that I am! Who will deliver me from this body of death?" (Rom. 7:15-24).

That is, we are not saved either from sin or for goodness by sheer effort. If I am digging a ditch, or building a house, or selling Fuller brushes, the success will be roughly proportional to the man-hours of energy which I put into it. But if I am interested in developing a Christlike

[1] Quoted by permission of Muriel Lester.

character I find that another set of factors enters in. I do not become humble, for instance, by trying to be humble. A humility sired by effort is counterfeit; a truly humble person is unaware that he is humble. A love that one has to work at, or that one strives for as an obligation, is spurious. I don't want anyone loving me out of a sense of duty! The only love worthy of the name is spontaneous. One does not purchase peace of mind by effort, else we would all have it. The New Testament speaks of "the peace which passes understanding." It defies nicely calculated formulas of thought and will. No one ever became happy by resolving to be happy. A certain cartoon in *Punch* awhile ago portrayed a huge, bemuscled mother letting out a little wart of a son onto the beach, and as she takes her leave of him, she says, "Johnny, you enjoy yourself, or I'll smack you!" But no one ever enjoyed himself on orders! Spiritual qualities, far from being the product of effort, are like our shadows; they follow us as we flee from them.

If we do not save ourselves spiritually by effort, how is it done? Paul's answer is contained in a crucial sentence in Romans 3:23-25. "Since all have sinned and fall short of the glory of God, they are justified by his grace as a gift, through the redemption which is in Christ Jesus, whom God put forward as an expiation by his blood, to be received by faith." There are four key words in this passage:

Justified. This word Paul borrowed from the law courts. When a man was haled before the bar of justice, if the judge, upon the evidence, pronounced him innocent of a crime and restored him to his rights as a citizen, the judge was said to "justify" him. He acquits him of the charge against him; the prisoner is granted amnesty. The Jews conceived of God as a cosmic Judge. Every man must sooner or later appear before the bar of God and hear the final words, "Guilty," or "Not Guilty." Paul's argument, as we have seen, is that all men are guilty of sin, and that no man by his unaided effort can ever attain deliverance. If a man ever gains acquittal, it will not have been earned by his own righteousness but will be a status God has conferred on him.

Paul employs other figures of speech to convey the same notion of passage from guilt to acquittal. He likens it to the emancipation of a slave from his master's power (Rom. 6:15-23). We were slaves to sin, but God has set us free. He also compares it to a widow after the death of her husband. A person was married, as it were, to sin, but sin has now died, and she is free to belong to another husband, even Christ (Rom. 7:1-6).

It should be plain what Paul is groping after. He is trying to make intelligible what had happened to him that day on the road to Damascus. He had set out on that journey with a bitter and grievous burden which had been the problem of long, haunting years. God through Christ had met him there. Despite his sin, God had pronounced him "Not Guilty." God had accepted him, blotted out the record, annulled the charges against him. But he had not earned forgiveness himself; *God had done it.* And if the human race is to be emancipated from its burden of wrongdoing, Paul felt that it would be, as with him, by the saving act of God alone.

Grace. Now this forgiveness which the Apostle experienced was an act of divine grace, an unmerited favor from God's hand. Paul had been reared in the stern tradition of the Pharisees which taught that men reap what they sow. His was a God who never gave men more than they earned, and who had decreed that the final wage of sin is death. Paul was a sinner. He had not been able to keep the Law. He had fiendishly persecuted God's people. Although he deserved punishment, God had rewarded him with kindness. Even though he had not been lovable, God had loved him. Paul discovered firsthand that just as God sends his rain on the evil and the good, so he offers all the things most worth having, including his salvation, to men who merit anything but kindness. God had not only stayed the hand of his punishment; he had heaped coals of fire on Paul's head by actually entrusting him with his gospel. As he wrote in the previous letter to the Ephesians, "To me, though I am the very least of all the saints, this grace was given, to preach to the Gentiles the unsearchable riches of Christ" (Eph. 3:8). That he, the chief of sinners, should have been made an Apostle filled his soul with breathless wonder. It caused him to reorganize his thought and life.

We, too, are the recipients of divine grace. Benjamin Franklin once said that a man who would demand a farm as a reward for giving a cup of cold water to a thirsty fellow on a hot day would be modest in his demands when compared with the man who looks for Heaven as a reward for his poor performance in the moral world. We all have sinned and fallen short of what God expects us to be, and yet God promises nevertheless his forgiveness, his mercy, his grace.

Expiation. The chief manifestation of this "grace" was for Paul the death of Christ on the cross. The Apostle accepted the premise of all ancient religion: that deliverance from sin can come only at the cost of sacrifice. If God forgave indiscriminately what incentive would there be for moral living? Why not go on sinning? God will forgive. That would shake down the whole moral edifice. The ancients held that God asked a blood offering as propitiation—a pigeon, a lamb, or a calf. Paul taught that the Christian religion surpassed every other faith in that it laid on the altar of forgiveness not a fowl or a beast but the very Lamb of God Himself.

Along with this principle Paul accepted another axiom of his time and world—the fact of human solidarity. In primitive society the tribe or the community was the real entity, rather than the individual. When one member sinned by breaking a taboo, all members of the clan shared in his guilt. When one triumphed over a foe, the victory belonged equally to the whole group. In similar fashion Paul taught that when Adam sinned every member of the human race fell with him. But, just as truly, when Christ satisfied the demands of God by offering his blood, when he died on the cross and then rose triumphantly over sin and the grave, the whole human species arose to eternal life with him. Read Romans 5:12 through 6:14 for Paul's argument.

A modern man finds it difficult to follow Paul's thinking, because he makes so many presuppositions that we do not accept. That does not mean, however, that the Cross is of no avail for us. We rationalize it differently. That is all. The Cross is for us not a price which Christ paid to the demands of God's righteousness and thus bought off—expiated—our guilt. The Cross is a moving portrait of God's love. When we lay hold of it imaginatively, applying it to our condition, it still has a marvelous power to save.

I recall once hearing Roland Hayes, the famous Negro tenor, sing the old spiritual, "An' He never said a mumbelin' word." He told in a word of preface that he got the song from his grandfather, an African chieftain, who had been pressed into slavery. When sometimes the sun was unbearably hot, the cotton row intolerably long, bitterness flamed in his heart, and the impulse to avenge or kill laid hold of him, he found his help in thinking of his Master.

> *They led Him up to Calvary's hill,*
> *An' He never said a mumbelin' word,*
> *They nail'd Him to the tree,*
> *An' He never said a mumbelin' word,*
> *Not a word, not a word, not a word.*
>
> *They pierced Him in the side*
> *An' He never said a mumbelin' word,*
> *He bowed his head and died.*
> *An' He never said a mumbelin' word,*
> *Not a word, not a word, not a word.*[1]

The remembrance of his Lord's suffering stilled his rebellious heart. So men of every race and class have grasped

[1] Negro spiritual, arranged by William Arms Fisher in "The Crucifixion," copyrighted 1926 by Oliver Ditson Company. Used by permission.

the Cross and found their sins not only theologically, but actually, taken away.

Faith. Finally, in addition to all that God has done to save us from sin there must be cooperation on our human part. God will not save me from my selfishness, if I insist on having my own way in all things. He will not save me from my ignorance, if I refuse to learn. He will not save me from my sinful pride, if I insist on looking downward instead of upward in my comparisons. God will not save a civilization, if it does not want to be saved. As one of our ablest theologians has phrased it, God can create creatures; He does not create sons. That is, God can make bodies, just as He makes rocks and trees. But He does not make men trust, love, or enjoy filial fellowship with Him. That rests with them. As every parent knows, it is one thing to bring children into the world and quite another thing, once they reach the age of independence, to get them to obey or share their lives with us.

Now "faith" is the human counterpart to God's grace. Grace is God reaching down to us; faith is man reaching up to take God's hand. Faith is saying Yes to the overtures of God. Faith is our cooperation with God's purposes. A man once asked the late Doctor Merton S. Rice what "Amen" meant at the end of a prayer. Doctor Rice replied whimsically, "It means, O. K., Lord, I'll bear my share of the expenses!" Faith is man's wholehearted response to God's efforts to save him. Faith begins with accepting the promises of God in Christ. It starts with belief that Christ is God's Son, that God has conquered Satan through him, and that if we will follow Christ we will be saved. But faith eventuates in our throwing ourselves in utter self-abandonment upon His promises to the point of bearing our share of the cost. Like the swimmer who leaps upon the breast of the stream, like the parachutist who plunges out into the open sky, hoping that his 'chute will not fail, so in faith we cast ourselves upon the mercies of God, trusting that He will bear us up.

Let me put Paul's conception of salvation by faith in an analogy. Suppose I have an internal physical ailment which calls for an operation. There are three courses open. First, I may refuse absolutely to permit an operation. The consequences will be that I suffer and eventually die. Or secondly, I may perform an operation on myself. If the malady is not too deep-seated, if my nerve holds out, if I have plenty of luck, I may conceivably succeed. There is a third alternative, however. In yonder city is a specialist in my particular malady. I believe in him so strongly that I go to his hospital, place myself under his care, and trustfully allow him to cut away the diseased tissue that threatens my life, thus doing for me what I am helpless to achieve by myself.

Similarly, as I confront my sins, if I stubbornly cling to them and resist the advances of God, He will let me take the consequences. That is what Paul calls "the wrath of God." If I try to perform a moral operation on myself, I can make some progress, but deep-seated trouble cannot be eliminated by human effort, as Paul's experience with the Law revealed. But there is the third alternative. I can yield in faith to the Great Physician, permitting him to effect in me those changes of heart and mind which we call salvation from sin. This last, in the form of a parable, is "justification by faith."

THE LIFE OF THE SPIRIT

Read Romans 8:4-33; 12:1-15; 13:1. Salvation by faith leads to the life of the Spirit. There are three levels at which men live. There is, first, the life of the flesh, the life of desire. A great segment of the human race tries to live by what it wants to do. Then there is the higher life of those who live "under the Law." They are the people who endeavor to live by conscience. Paul before Damascus was one of their number. Finally, there is the still higher state when men live by the Spirit. God is in control of their lives. A recent newspaper columnist, commenting on his addiction to the tobacco habit, wrote, "I don't smoke cigarettes. Cigarettes smoke me." Well, just as habit may rule us, so Spirit may also govern. Paul says, "It is no longer I who live, but Christ who lives in me" (Gal. 2:20). This is the state of spiritual living. A man is not truly saved until he reaches the place where God takes over.

The phrase which Paul uses to describe this state is one quoted repeatedly in Romans—"in Christ." Paul thought of God's Spirit as Christ himself, liberated after the resurrection, let loose in the world, and ready to enter into direct fellowship with the Christian. To be "in Christ" means to be in communion with the Spirit of Christ. It means giving heed to the Christ within us. It involves examining all moral questions by asking, Does this hurt my relationship to Jesus Christ? Is it unworthy of Him?

It means accepting His help as we face the world and the flesh and the devil. The Law had told Paul what he ought to do; it had not helped him to perform it. Against this impotence of the Law he sets the glorious moral power of the Spirit: "I can do all things in him who strengthens me" (Phil. 4:13).

This life in Christ involves complete subjection of the personality to the Lord. It means thinking Christ's thoughts after him, what Paul calls "the mind of Christ" (I Cor. 2:16). It obviously includes Christlike conduct. Beneath the Christian exterior are Christian feelings. How many there are in the world, to use Galsworthy's phrase, who are engaged in "flogging dead horses on a journey to the moon," playing the game but with uninspired hearts! When the Spirit controls, it makes our emotions alive. Spiritual living even encompasses the subconscious. One of the questions John Wesley addressed to his preachers was, "Can we make our dreams holy?" The saved life is one in which the whole personality—mind, will, feelings, and the subconscious—are in thralldom to Jesus Christ.

The life of the spirit is *characterized by peace, hope, and love:*

PEACE. "Therefore, since we are justified by faith, we have peace with God through our Lord Jesus Christ" (Rom. 5:1). Once faith possesses us we stop fighting God. The hostility which formerly marked our conduct and estranged us from Him is removed. The fears which kept alive our antagonism to God are swept away by the vision He gave us of the Father. *When we get on right terms with Him, the fundamental tension which has run hitherto through all life is relaxed*. Best of all, *as things become right without, peace ensues within*. As when the lineman cuts our domestic line into the central power system the lights at once come on, the heat comes up, the water pump begins to throb, and the radio starts to sing; *so right relations with the Lord of the universe around us, mean joy, poise, and inner serenity of the world within*.

The peace which Paul found in Christ was not the peace of animal contentment, the peace of the cow that fills herself with clover and lies down in the shade to chew her cud. It was not the peace of stagnation of the pool, sheltered from the winds that blow, untroubled by the mad currents of the mountain stream. His was the peace which sprang from a certain relationship, supreme and everlasting: "Who shall separate us from the love of Christ? Shall tribulation, or distress, or persecution, or famine, or nakedness, or peril, or sword? . . . No, in all these things we are more than conquerors through him who loved us. For I am sure that neither death, nor life, nor angels, nor principalities, nor things present, nor things to come, nor powers, nor height, nor depth, nor anything else in all creation, will be able to separate us from the love of God in Christ Jesus our Lord." (Rom. 8:35, 37-39). Paul had lived a life of strain and stress, but through it all he took the consciousness that Christ was with him, and through it all he dwelt, to use the beautiful phrase of the mystics, "in a multitude of peace."

Hope. "We know that the whole creation has been groaning in travail together until now; and not only the creation, but we ourselves, who have the first fruits of the

Spirit, groan inwardly as we wait for adoption as sons, the redemption of our bodies. For in this hope we were saved" (Rom. 8:22-24).

Paul was no Pollyanna. He did not blink at brutal facts. "The whole creation has been groaning together until now." The Apostle looked out on nature and heard her dirge of sorrow. He must have thought of the rapacity of the animal world, the ruthless trampling upon plant life, the catastrophes of flood and earthquake and fire. In his imagination he heard the ceaseless sobbing of the sea. He caught the moaning of the Church in her troubles. It seemed to him that the world was like a young life, crying as a woman cries in childbirth for release from pain. Yet, here the Christian apostle differs from the pagan pessimist. The latter hears the anguish of the world and at best can only sympathize. Paul is equally alive to the pain, but for him it is big with promise. For out of the travail of the world God's family will be born upon the earth. Paul's outlook is one of hope, because the pains of the present hour are prophetic of a fulfillment to come.

Paul Elmer More, the distinguished literary critic, once wrote that the great contribution of Christianity to the world was not love, as we so often assume, but hope.[1] For why be loving, if in the end there is not hope? It is very chivalrous, of course, to say that we ought to be kind and generous, no matter what the outcome may be. But the natural man does not follow that logic. The great service of Christianity to the world is its message that in the face of the blatant power of evil there is hope for those who put their faith in love.

98

[1] Paul Elmer More, *Sceptical Approach to Religion* (Princeton: Princeton University Press, 1934), p. 183.

Why may we have hope? The immediate reason is what we have already realized. Paul says, in the passage quoted above, that Christians "have the first fruits of the Spirit," literally, "the first installment of the gift of the Spirit." *A person who has himself been redeemed by Christ knows that what God has done for him He can do for anyone else.* If He can do it for others, then the future of the world is bright with promise. The very possession now of spiritual qualities is itself an earnest of yet better things to come. If God can here and now raise us from the death of sin to the life of righteousness, we have every ground for believing that He can raise up the physical body when death has overtaken it.

Underlying the guarantee of hope, of course, is the nature and existence of God Himself. "We know that in everything God works for good with those who love him, who are called according to his purpose" (Rom. 8:28). The resources and compassion of the infinite God are available for our use. In a sense the King James translation brings out the meaning better: "All things work together for good to them that love God" (A.V.). Not everything is initially good, but it "can work together" for good. Not everything in its isolation is good, but taken in the perspective of the whole of life it is. I once heard Bishop McConnell preach on this text, and he used the analogy of a ship. "If you should take each single part of an ocean-going steamer," he said—"the steel ribs, the keel, the rudder, the mast, the wireless—and drop it into the sea, it would sink. But if these are fashioned together into a whole, we have a vessel which defies the buffeting of the waves. So many a solitary experience in life will 'sink' us, but when we take life as a whole we see God's hand in it and find it tolerable."

But Paul is most hopeful, because God has predestined us to salvation; "those whom he foreknew he also predestined to be conformed to the image of his Son, in order that he might be the first-born among many brethren. And those whom he predestined he also called; and those whom he called he also justified; and those whom he justified he also glorified" (Rom. 8:29-30).

"Predestination" makes a jarring sound in a Methodist ear. Several points are to be considered, however. First of all, Paul is not a consistent predestinationist. Our Methodist forebears were right when they insisted that, if God pulls the strings of our lives, we are puppets. Moral responsibility vanishes. But Paul recognizes the fact of moral accountability as we shall see later in this chapter. In Romans 1:18 and 2:1 he says that we are without excuse for our sinfulness, while in Romans 10 he indicts his own beloved Israel for rejecting Christ. "Work out your own salvation," he tells the Philippians (2:12). What Paul is doing in Romans 8:29-30 is to draw implications from his own experience. He set out to be a persecutor of Christians and a Power greater than himself had seized him, turned him around, and made an apostle of him. He had not chosen God so much as God had chosen him! Paul stands in wonder before what had happened. He never tried to harmonize his own experience with another fact which he recognized equally well; namely, that we are morally responsible beings.

Furthermore, we must place Paul in the framework of his age. He lived in a day when men believed that human destiny is controlled by the stars. If you were born with a certain horoscope, your fate was irrevocably fixed. Against this feeling of domination by a ruthless mechanical fate Paul bravely declared that our days are in the keeping of a loving God.

Again, we must recall that we can hold to Paul's notion of God's sovereignty with regard to our ultimate destiny without destroying the power of immediate choice. What Paul is saying is that *God is going to arrive*. His kingdom shall be established. We are free either to oppose His purposes or to cooperate. If we resist God's plans, frustration and final defeat will be our lot. To employ the figure of the philosopher, William James, God is like a master playing chess with a novice. The beginner is free to make any move he will, but the master foresees all the possibilities and can checkmate them all.[1] So God's plans will not be overthrown by perverse or sinful men. *If, however, we choose to cooperate with God's plans, our lives will be full of peace, joy, and increasing fulfilment.*

After all, what is freedom? Surely not the power to do whatever one wants. No human being has that power. Freedom is perception of where Almighty God is going, willingly making His purposes the goal of our existence, and marching victoriously with Him toward the blessedness He has in store for His faithful children. This is Paul's deeper meaning, however much his words may seem to contradict it.

LOVE. Finally, the life of the spirit eventuates in right

[1] William James, "The Dilemma of Determinism," in his *Essays on Faith and Morals* (New York; Longmans Green & Co., 1943), p. 181.

relations not only with God (peace) and toward the future (hope) but with one's fellows (love). "I appeal to you therefore, brethren, by the mercies of God, to present your bodies as a living sacrifice, holy and acceptable to God, which is your spiritual worship" (Rom. 12:1). Since God himself is Love, our response must be loving, as the word "sacrifice" suggests, utter self-abandonment and self-consecration. *Love,* the Letter to the Romans emphasizes, *means the promotion of peace in all the relations of life:*

Within the church: Read Romans 12:3-13. Love is the willing subordination of individual gifts to the welfare of the whole, a point Paul makes at great length in his Letter to the Corinthians. Love means, too, warm affection, courtesy—"outdo one another in showing honor"—(12:10), unceasing prayer (12:12), charity—"Contribute to the needs of the saints"—and open-handed hospitality (12, 13).

Toward one's enemies: Read Romans 12:14-21. *Love means not revenge,* which the Old Testament had permitted, not mere non-resistance, *but drowning evil in an overplus of good.* "Bless (literally, "speak well of") those who persecute you; . . . Repay no one evil for evil, . . . never avenge yourselves, but leave it to the wrath of God; . . . 'if your enemy is hungry, feed him; if he is thirsty, give him drink'. . . . Do not be overcome by evil, but overcome evil with good."

Toward the state: Read Romans 13:1-7. Love requires loyalty to the government. Paul regarded the state as providentially ordained of God, else it could not exist. Resistance to the state is evil. (Remember that Paul is talking of the state in general, which is on the side of good. He gives no guidance when, as we have seen in recent years, a particular state becomes an instrument for evil.) Christians are scrupulously to render unto Caesar the things that are Caesar's.

Toward those of tender conscience: Love prescribes respect. Read Romans 14:1-23. As we indicated earlier, the Roman Church was a mixed group, containing Gentiles, who were very liberal in their practice ("the strong") and Jews who kept dietary laws (14:2) and religious holidays (14:5) strictly ("the weak"). Paul counsels kindly regard and abstention from censorious judgment (14:3-5, 10, 13), for he knew that a civilized community rests on respect for conscience, even though it be mistaken or over-scrupulous. He reminds all that although we are not accountable for some of our deeds to one another, in the end we are accountable for all of our deeds—not to one another but to God (14:10-12). In general, those who are strong should "bear with"—that is, not merely tolerate but actually suffer deprivations for—the failings of the weak, following in the footsteps of Christ, who had not pleased himself (15:1-3).

ISRAEL'S REJECTION

Read Romans 9:1 through 11:36. The Jews from the earliest times had prided themselves on being a chosen people; they rejoiced in having been selected by God over their enemies, the Ishmaelites and Edomites. But now God had apparently handed over to the Gentiles the salvation first offered to the Jews. Paul, loyal Hebrew that he was, anguishes over it. "My conscience bears me witness in the Holy Spirit," he says, "that I have great sorrow and unceasing anguish in my heart. For I could wish that I myself were accursed and cut off from Christ for the sake of my brethren, my kinsmen by race" (9:1-3). How is this sore fact that Israel seems no longer to be God's chosen race to be met? Romans 9:11 is Paul's solution to the problem.

To begin with, the Apostle insists that God never did choose all of Israel for His inheritance. Read Romans 9:6-13. "For not all who are descended from Israel belong to Israel, and not all are children of Abraham because they are his descendants." The true "Israel" is a spiritual community, and God's promise of salvation applies to them.

Furthermore, God is an absolute sovereign. Read Romans 9:14-24. His is the power and right to dispose of human affairs in His own way: "So then he has mercy upon whomever he wills, and he hardens the heart of whomever he wills" (9:18). If I do not like it, who am I, ". . . a man, to answer back to God? Will what is molded say to the molder, 'Why have you made me thus?' Has the potter no right over the clay, to make out of the same lump one vessel for beauty and another for menial use?" See Romans 9:20-21.

Then, too, the Jews merit God's rejection of them, because they rejected Him. Read Romans 9:30 through 10:21. When the Messiah came, they did not accept him. They had zeal but lacked spiritual understanding. They wanted to be saved, but they went about it in the wrong way, through the Law instead of by faith. The Jews in Paul's eyes were a disobedient people and God rejected them for their disobedience.

Still, God's rejection of Israel is only partial. Read Romans 11:1-33. "So too at the present time there is a remnant," a select few among the Jews, "chosen by grace" (Rom. 11:5). Further, His rejection is only temporary 11:11-25). In God's Providence Israel rejected the Gospel in order that the Gentiles might have it, so that the Jew, moved by jealousy at the sight of his own possession in the hands of others, would accept what he now rejects. The time is coming, Paul confidently asserts, when Israel shall be united in the Church of God (11:26). This vision of God's final goodness to His beloved nation, the contrast between the apparent injustice and the real justice of God, causes Paul to burst forth in a great ascription of praise with which this chapter may appropriately close: "O the depth of the riches and wisdom and knowledge of God!" See Romans 11:33.

V

THE PROBLEMS OF
THE CHURCH

Corin-
-thians

V

Corinth and its church. The early Church had not only a philosophy and a message. It had problems! The difficulties of a Christian community come to their most vivid expression in the letters of Paul to the Christians of Corinth. The city, situated on the isthmus connecting the Peloponnesus, the southern peninsula of Greece, with the mainland, drew its population from all points of the compass. Though basically Greek, it was the residence of the Roman proconsul and his large Italian retinue. Inevitably, this city, which stood at the gateway between East and West, also had a large Oriental population. Its main source of livelihood, the transportation industry, employed thousands of sailors and longshoremen.

The problems of the church at Corinth were occasioned not only by the polyglot citizenry of a seaside town but by the immorality of its people, which was a byword even in those dissolute times. The world-famous temple of Aphrodite, towering above the city, boasted a thousand sacred prostitutes. Sanctuaries in honor of Serapis and Isis, Oriental mystery religions, decorated the chief corners. Wandering prophets of a thousand bizarre sects preached profligate doctrines and peddled their salacious wares. Corinth was drenched with sex and idolatry, which accounts for the fact that so much of the space in the letters is devoted to these themes.

Paul had first visited the city around A.D. 50. After a ministry in Athens which was largely unsuccessful, where the Apostle's austere gospel had failed to dent the cultural sophistication of the Greek capital, Paul moved on to Corinth, where he remained more than eighteen months. The Acts of the Apostles, our chief source, gives us little information about his stay. We learn that he roomed with a Jewish couple, Aquila and Priscilla, who had been expelled from Rome by an edict of the Emperor Claudius (Acts 18:2-3). They were colleagues in the tent-making profession, as well as fellow countrymen of Paul. They worked their trade together. Paul adopted his usual strategy of preaching in the synagogue and seems to have drawn off some of the faithful, as well as proselytes and hangers-on of the Jewish community. The account in Acts (18:5 ff.) seems to indicate that the Jews forced Paul out of the synagogue into a private house nearby. But success marked his ministry, otherwise he probably would not have remained for a year and a half. The fact that Crispus, the ruler of the Corinthian synagogue, became one of Paul's converts (Acts 18:8) witnesses to Paul's effectiveness. When he left the city of Corinth a strong church remained behind, eventually one of the most important centers of the early Christian movement.

The membership of the Corinthian Church apparently represented a cross section of the motley populace among which it was founded. Although it was predominantly Gentile, a Jewish constituency was also present. Many of the members belonged to the lower strata of society in which the seaport town abounded, including slaves, sailors, dock laborers, and petty tradesmen. Some of the women who played an important role in the church had been people of loose morals and had carried their freedom from convention into the church meetings (I Cor. 11:2-16). The upper classes, however, were not unrepresented. Chloe (I Cor. 1:11) was probably well-to-do, since her slaves sought out Paul. Gaius (I Cor. 1:14 and Rom. 16:23), a man of means, offered the hospitality of his home to the whole church. Crispus, ruler of the synagogue (Acts 18:8), and Erastus, the city treasurer (Rom. 16:23), also belonged to the fellowship.

PAUL'S LETTERS TO THE CORINTHIANS

The New Testament formally lists two letters of Paul to the Christians of Corinth. Actually, there were four. The two letters which we have in our Bible are a patchwork of twice that number. We must remember that the Apostle's letters were not Scripture for the early Church; the Old Testament was their Bible. They were just letters preserved on scrolls by different churches and individuals. Some time after the Apostle's death, the churches, sensing the importance of his writings, began collecting his letters. They lacked our modern sense of precise sequence and order; the task of copying was costly and the need of utilizing every inch of the precious papyrus on which the letters had been written was consequently great. Hence their tendency was to run all the material together. One of the fascinating bits of detective work performed by modern scholars has been to unscramble the parts of four different letters, glued together somewhere in history, into "First and Second Corinthians."

The sequence of Paul's letters to the Corinthians runs somewhat as follows:

After ministering to the Corinthians for a year and a half, Paul made a quick trip to Jerusalem, taking Aquila and Priscilla with him as far as Ephesus. On his return to Ephesus he found that his two friends had won a notable convert for the faith, a learned and eloquent Alexandrian Jew named Apollos. So impressed were they with his gifts that they sent Apollos back to Corinth to carry on Paul's work, while the Apostle entered on a three-year ministry at Ephesus. While Paul's work bore fruit in this great city of Asia Minor, he was eaten with anxiety for Corinth. Rumors reaching him of division and of an invasion of worldliness in the body of the church led him to write to the Corinthians a severe letter of rebuke. See I Corinthians 5:9 for a reference to the letter which, except for the fragment contained in II Corinthians 6:14 through 7:1, has been lost. It is this lost letter which is the real "First" Corinthians.

The Corinthians, answering his letter, sought his advice on several moral questions. At about the time that their reply reached Paul, word came to him of quarreling which had broken out among the brethren (I Cor. 1:11). The letter written by the Corinthians, with its various questions, is now entirely lost, but Paul's answer to it has been preserved and is our First Corinthians. The first four chapters deal with the rumored disunion in the Church. The remainder are devoted to a discussion, one after another, of the queries which his Corinthian friends had raised.

Paul's reply (I Cor.), however, did not halt the trouble. The cliquishness, intellectual pride, and neglect of common morality for which Corinth was famous became more pronounced, aggravated now by some of Paul's old enemies, the Judaizers, who insisted on squeezing the gospel into the straitjacket of Hebrew Law. Paul's troubles were further increased by the intelligence that the church had decided to shake off his authority altogether. He may have made a hurried visit; perhaps he sent one of his trusted lieutenants. At any rate, the answer was insult. Paul thereupon sat down in a bitter and indignant mood and asserted his claim to be an Apostle, and sought to shame the disloyal church into repentance. Scholars believe that II Corinthians 10 through 13 is a part of this letter, also long supposed to have been lost.

Paul apparently left Ephesus soon after, having sent his friend, Titus, ahead to explore the situation in Corinth. The Apostle waited anxiously at Philippi. Titus returned at last with the cheering news that the Corinthians were ashamed of their conduct and eager to welcome the Apostle. Whereupon Paul wrote a letter of joyous relief from an overflowing heart. This letter is our Second Corinthians 1 through 9. Complex as they were in their make-up, the Letters to the Corinthians are among the most treasured writings of the New Testament. To begin with, they contain two of the noblest chapters in all religious literature. One is I Corinthians 13, the most exquisite passage that Paul ever wrote—the matchless hymn to love. It appears in prose form in our Bible, but in loftiness of feeling and marching rhythm it is poetry of the highest order. The other great chapter is I Corinthians 15, Paul's magnificent statement on immortality.

The Letters to the Corinthians are not only priceless for their inspiration but are also of supreme historical value. They contain our earliest record of the Resurrection of Jesus. Though the Gospels stand first in the New Testament, I Corinthians 15:3-8, with its descriptions of the appearances of Christ to the disciples, was written almost twenty years earlier than the Gospel accounts. Paul gives a firsthand report of his vision of the risen Lord and grounds our faith on fact. These letters also supply our earliest account of the institution of the Lord's Supper (I Cor. 11:23-26). When we remember that Paul wrote less than twenty-five years after the Crucifixion, the importance of their testimony is evident.

We are indebted to the Corinthian Letters, furthermore, for the richest picture of life in the early church which we possess. It is a cinematic representation of the first Christians. We get a vivid look at their quarrels, their marriage practices, an early feminist movement, their likes and dislikes, the enigmas that puzzled their consciences, their worship, and their response to their great leader, Paul. The letters are the most important sources of information in the Bible as to the way the early Christians thought and lived.

Again, these letters show us how to perform a task which every generation must fulfill for itself: how to apply the timeless principles of Christ's teachings to the timely problems of the hour. Paul had a wonderful gift for seizing a contemporary difficulty and holding it up for the eternal light of the gospel to play upon. With wonderful insight he lays hold of a minor issue and runs it back to a guiding principle, showing how the counsels of Jesus, valid for the peasants of Galilee, were just as vital for the complex civilization of a Gentile city. How much he has to teach us as we seek to make Christ's teaching live in our day!

This chapter is entitled "The Problems of the Church," and rightly, for the Church has always had difficulties to meet, in the early days even more than now. Doctor Kirsopp Lake, famous New Testament scholar at Harvard, used to say, "It must be a great comfort to any Christian minister today to realize that no matter how bad his parish may be, the one which Saint Paul had in Corinth was worse!" If our plight is better than Paul's it is due in part to his courageous and enlightened handling of the situations he faced. Across the centuries the Church has drawn wisdom from Paul as well as from its own years of growth and experience. After all, *a church is not a museum* for the exhibition of finished saints. *It is a training school in Christian character, and our best educators tell us that we learn by solving problems.* In this chapter we shall take up, one by one, the problems which bothered the Corinthians and endeavor to look at the Christian solution through the eyes of the great Christian after Christ.

THE PROBLEM OF FACTIONS IN THE CHURCH. Read I Corinthians 1:10 through 4:21. "For it has been reported to me," says Paul, "that there is quarreling among you, my brethren. What I mean is that each one of you says, 'I belong to Paul,' or 'I belong to Apollos,' or 'I belong to Cephas,' or 'I belong to Christ' " (I Cor. 1:11-12). That is, the church members were divided into parties. Some were lined up behind Paul; others behind Apollos, who had succeeded Paul; still others were loyal to Cephas (Peter); presumably these were Jewish Christians; and some called themselves the "Christ-party." Probably these last were rebels against Paul, men who felt that Christ belonged to them and not to the Apostle.

This is, unfortunately, not the last church quarrel stemming from a similar cause: some members favor one pastor over against another! These civil wars in a congregation are always tragic, for they not only belie our Christian profession of love, but no church ever came out of one without injury to itself and to the Master's cause. How does Paul handle the dispute?

He gets at the heart of it by reminding the Corinthians that they are thinking too highly of themselves. Most trouble in a community arises from neurotic self-centeredness. The Corinthians were bordering on it. They had put men, themselves and human teachers, in place of Christ.

"Let him who boasts," says Paul, "boast of the Lord" (I Cor. 1:31). After all, the Apostle asks devastatingly, "What have you that you did not receive? If then you received it, why do you boast as if it were not a gift?" See I Corinthians 4:7. All they knew about the gospel they had taken from their spiritual parents, and now they were presuming to sit in judgment on them! It was like babies criticizing their mothers' milk! God alone, Paul reminds them, has the right to judge (I Cor. 4:4). The followers of Apollos, especially, had preened themselves on their "wisdom." (Apollos came from Alexandria, the famous seat of philosophy.) They had set up the "wisdom" of men against God. See I Corinthians 1:18 through 2:5. The Christian message, Paul reminds them, is not "wisdom," an intellectual system of beliefs, but the Cross, which seems like foolishness to men but actually is a divine power of salvation to those who live by it (1:18). And the Apostle adds slyly that, if they were really as wise as they counted themselves to be, really mature, and genuinely Christian, they would not have got into the mess they were in (I Cor. 3:1-4).

Paul goes on to say that he, Apollos, Cephas, and others who had ministered to the church were not competitors but co-workers. "I planted, Apollos watered, but God gave the growth. . . . For we are fellow workmen for God" (I Cor. 3:6, 9). The Corinthians are not required to choose between their pastors, because "all are yours; and you are Christ's; and Christ is God's" (I Cor. 3:22-23).

But Paul does not stop with logic. He proceeds to shame the Corinthians a bit. He contrasts their comfortable, self-satisfied, complacent life with the sort of existence the apostles had known—sentenced to death in the arena, hungry and thirsty, "ill-clad and buffeted and homeless," doing hand labor, reviled, persecuted, slandered, and becoming as refuse and offscouring in the eyes of the world (I Cor. 4:8-13). Then he concludes: they may have had many guides, but he was their only father in the gospel. If they kept up their quarreling he would bring a stick with him when he came—and use it. See I Corinthians 4:14-21.

A PROBLEM OF IMMORALITY IN THE CHURCH. Read I Corinthians 5:1-13; 6:9-20. Word had come to Paul of a case of incest. A prominent member of the church was living with his father's wife in a married relationship. Both Roman and Jewish law forbade it, the latter upon penalty of death. What disturbed the Apostle was not only the fact that this sort of thing was going on within the bosom of the church—very likely it was a solitary case—but the attitude which the Corinthians were taking toward it. "You are arrogant!" Paul says. "Ought you not rather to mourn?" The community was accepting the moral laxity as a matter of course; no one's conscience seemed bothered by it.

Paul's high moral consciousness boils over. Read I Corinthians 5:3 and 11-13; also 6:6-10. "Kick this fellow out of the church at once," he orders. "Do not associate with any one who . . . is guilty of immorality; . . . not even to eat with such a person. . . . Do not be deceived; neither the immoral, nor idolaters, nor adulterers, nor homosexuals, nor thieves, nor the greedy, nor drunkards, nor revilers, nor robbers will inherit the kingdom of God."

Sexual immorality is for Paul a sin against one's body, and therefore an offense against God, whose temple it is (I Cor. 6:15-20). When a person indulges in obscene practices he merges his personality with his partner in vice and thus defiles the very shrine of God to whom the body belongs. What a lift to human morality were we to catch this thought of Paul's of our bodies as sacred!

As usual, Paul is thinking of the effect of the incident, not only on the individuals involved, but on the community. He fears the terrific consequences such a breach of ethics may have on the ideals of the church. He likens it to yeast in the dough, which will soon spread to the whole (I Cor. 5:6-8). If he were writing today he would probably talk about the rotten apple in the barrel, or, worse, about cancer in the body. A moral infection never stops where it begins. The ideals, if not the conduct, of a society are weakened when it allows a flagrant case of immorality to go unchecked.

Paul is stern. Sometimes the religious conscience has been excessively cruel, as when the Puritans whipped moral delinquents on the commons of their villages. Still, enlightened judgment would support the Apostle. The Church can compromise with some things—with ignorance, stupidity, lukewarmness, apostasy. But no church can wink at sexual sin and keep its own integrity or hold the respect of its community.

THE QUESTION OF LITIGATION BETWEEN CHRISTIANS. Read I Corinthians 6:1-18. Again the question had arisen as to the position Christians should take on the matter of lawsuits. Apparently it had come to Paul's notice that some members of the Church were involved in a dispute about property, or breach of contract. They had gone to court about it. What was the Christian attitude?

Paul has two observations to make. First, a Christian who feels himself obliged to go to court betrays a defect in his Christianity. He has already lost his real case—for litigation itself is a sign that the litigant is more willing to inflict injury on others than to suffer it himself. When he sues a fellow-Christian, he demonstrates clearly that under provocation he no longer possesses the spirit of loving-kindness and patient good will which the Master enjoined (I Cor. 6:7-8).

Furthermore, a lawsuit between Christians is a reflection on the greatness of the Church itself (I Cor. 6:1-6). Are not one's Christian brethren capable of arbitrating disputes between members? Paul feels about lawsuits in a church the way we feel when two brothers in the same family go to court with one another. We believe that somehow they should get together about the family table and adjust their differences rather than wash their linen in public.

THE PROBLEM OF MARRIAGE AND DIVORCE. Read I Corinthians 7; II Corinthians 6:14 through 7:1. Then the inevitable question of marriage comes up. The Corinthians were especially at sea on the subject. On the one hand, there were those who had grown up in the sex-drenched city and who had become accustomed to the loose standards to which we have referred. Not a few of the Christians themselves had kept mistresses or had been prostitutes before their conversion, and that experience dimmed their outlook on marriage. At the other extreme there were those who, reacting to the immorality of the times, felt that everything connected with sex was vile and that marriage was a sin. Some of the converts were still bound to pagans whom they had married in their pre-Christian days. Were they to divorce husbands and wives who did not share Christian ideals of marriage, or were they to live with them? There were libertines in the Church who believed that when Christ superseded the Law of Moses the Seventh Commandment went out with the rest. The whole situation was beclouded by the conviction that the Lord was very soon to return and the world come to stop. Under the circumstances, should one marry or not? These are the knotty queries with which the Corinthians confronted Paul.

The Apostle's advice may be summed up in three or four propositions: To begin with, he believed, personally, that to remain single is preferable to being married (I Cor. 7:1, 6). Paul is one of those individuals who, while warm of heart and passionate in his love of people, had very little sex interest. Indeed, he even appears to have depreciated sex and wished everybody were like himself.

Though exalting the single state, he goes on to affirm that it is better to marry than to be immoral. Frankly, it is better to marry than to be aflame with passion (I Cor. 7:9). If two engaged people fear that their desires for each other may go beyond control, let them marry (I Cor. 7:36-38). Paul is realistic enough to know that the average person is unfitted for celibate life. Rather than live in perpetual tension or indulge in sexual irregularities, let a person marry. Differing from the ultra-ascetics, Paul pronounces marriage no sin (I Cor. 7:28 and 38-40).

His advice, in view of the contemporary situation which confronted him was: stay the way you are. If you are married, do not seek to be free. If you are single, do not marry (I Cor. 7:27-29). If an unbeliever wants to stay with a Christian spouse, or vice versa, let them remain together (I Cor. 7:12-14). While Paul believes that a Christian should only marry a Christian (I Cor. 7:39), he can see values in a mixed marriage, if it already exists. It may result in the winning of a pagan husband or wife to the Lord (I Cor. 7:16). If the two of differing faiths can live peacefully it is to the children's advantage to have an unbroken home (I Cor. 7:14). In general, Paul invokes a quarantine on intimacies with pagans, because of what it tends to do to the Christian life (II Cor. 6:14, 17). Still, conversion represents for him essentially a radical change in the inner life. It need not overturn one's external life. Therefore, a Christian will not seek dissolution of his marriage any more than a slave will claim emancipation (I Cor. 7:20-24).

The general consensus of scholars is that Paul is not at his best when he counsels on marriage. His own marital life—if he had one—is curtained from our knowledge. Surely he has little appreciation of the comradeship of marriage—the union of two hearts in family affection, the clasp of two hands in play and work. He was living under the conviction that the world was about to end. Why marry or separate when, perhaps, by next Thursday, it will be all over? Further, he was trying to adjust marriage *mores* to a very wicked city, where sex solicitation beckoned to youth at every streetcorner. He was not painting the portrait of ideal marriage; his aim was to establish between man and woman a relation best adapted to circumstances which were not ideal.

THE PROBLEM OF OVERCONSCIENTIOUSNESS. Read I Corinthians 8:1 through 11:1. "Now concerning food offered to idols" (8:1), . . . In a pagan city such as Corinth much of the meat consumed by the public had been offered as a sacrifice on the altar of heathen gods before it was transported to market. The Jewish members of the church—those referred to as "the weak" (8:7), those of tender conscience—were troubled, having eaten only kosher food all their life. There were others, converts from paganism, who, when they sat down before a roast, suspected that the meat had previously done duty as a sacrifice. It brought back all their former pagan associations and made it harder to live a Christian life, just as it is difficult for the person in our days who has himself conquered liquor or tobacco to be forced into their presence. On the other hand, there were emancipated church members in Corinth—"the strong"—who ate this sacrificial meat without any scruples at all. What is a Christian's duty, they ask Paul, when faced by a situation of this sort?

First of all, the Apostle calls on "the weak," the over-conscientious, to be realistic. An idol is just an idol, and for a Christian an idol is nothing (I Cor. 8:4-6). The fact that meat has once been offered to a deity does not destroy its worth as food. In the eyes of the one true God whether we eat it or not does not matter (I Cor. 8:8).

Furthermore, Paul advises his readers to eat what is sold in the markets without inquiry (I Cor. 8:25). If one dines at an unbeliever's home he is *not* to ask embarrassing questions as to where the main dish came from (I Cor. 8:27).

There are people in every community who are easily offended no matter what problem may arise. They fuss over nonessential details, quibble over points that do not matter. Every now and then they need to be told the truth about themselves or they will only be encouraged in their whims and become still greater nuisances. After all, an idol is nothing. Our notions do not change reality.

On the other hand, Paul is quite as outspoken to the liberals who pride themselves on their ethical maturity. Granted that I know an idol is just an idol, still there are good Christians who look at it differently. Therefore, as a Christian I am bound to respect the other man's conscience, because it is authoritative for him. I'll be charitable. I'll not needlessly offend. I will cease eating meat, not because I think he is right, but because I love him and do not wish to hurt him. Paul shows his grand Christian spirit when he writes, "Therefore if food is a cause of my brother's falling, I will never eat meat" (I Cor. 8:13). Then he goes on to remind the "strong" brethren, how easy it is to fall back into idolatry if one trifles with it. Even their fathers had been guilty of backsliding (I Cor. 10:6-13). There has been many a person since who thought that he had a habit whipped—only to discover that his pride was his undoing.

Paul sums up the matter in one great principle: "Whether

you eat or drink, or whatever you do, do all to the glory of God" (I Cor. 10:31). Our only duty is to subordinate life and liberty to the love and glory of God. Paul urges his readers to give up haggling and wrangling over eating and drinking and fast days. A life of scruples is always weak, and scruples beget scruples until one's life is swallowed up in Pharisaism. "Love God," said Augustine rightly, "and do what you please." But the test of whether we are loving God is whether our conduct is helping rather than hindering others. So Paul can rephrase his principle in human terms to read: "Give no offense to Jews or to Greeks or to the church of God, just as I try to please all men in everything I do, not seeking my own advantage, but that of many, that they may be saved." (I Cor. 10:32-33). The ultimate moral equation is:

That is good = whatever pleases God = whatever helps men.

THE VEILING OF WOMEN. Read I Corinthians 11:2-16. Here is another problem which at first blush seems trivial. Apparently some of the women in the Corinthian church figured that Christianity represented a New Deal in religion. In Roman society men appeared with bared heads, symbolizing their status as lords and masters, while their women were not seen in public without head coverings, a symbol also of their position as men's inferiors. Converts to a new order of life, a few energetic feminists had turned up at church without hats or veils. What was to be done about it?

Paul is no more loath here about offering an opinion

than elsewhere: Let the women keep their heads covered in church! His arguments are not very convincing: As man reflects the glory of God, so woman reflects the glory of man, and should be dominated by him; women are inferior to men—what is appropriate for a man is not thereby correct for his wife; God created women to have more of a covering on their heads, i.e., hair, than men! The Apostle holds fast to the old-world view of male superiority.

Yet, there is method in his masculinity! He was jealous of the good name of the Church and its members. In Corinth only women of questionable reputation or admitted prostitutes functioned outside the home. No modest Greek woman ever appeared in public with head uncovered. Paul feared that, if the women members ignored the rules of etiquette in this matter, the door might be opened to a complete misunderstanding of Christian morals, especially since the pagans generally believed that the Christians indulged in sensual orgies at their "love-feasts."

MISBEHAVIOR AT THE LORD'S SUPPER. Read I Corinthians 11:17-34. The original "Lord's Supper" was not a liturgical service with worshipers coming forward to an altar to partake symbolically of a sip of wine and a pinch of bread. The first Lord's Supper was a church dinner, either paid for out of the treasury or provided by several members who brought food to the church, after the manner of our "covered-dish" meals. They ate and drank together in thankful remembrance of the Lord. But disorders had crept in. The common meal of general sharing had become "common" in the vulgar sense. The rich clannishly ate with their own set, and arranged to get there first and eat up the food, so that the poor and the latecomers stood about with empty stomachs and envious glances. And some had even gone to excess and become drunk at the Lord's table! See I Corinthians 11:21.

The Apostle's rebuke is swift. Such conduct is nothing less than sacrilege. He reminds them how the Lord had instituted the Supper as a memorial meal: "Do this in remembrance of me"—in remembrance not only of his sacrificial life and death but of the intimate fellowship which they had once known with him and hoped to enjoy again (I Cor. 11:24-26). Selfishness and drunkenness are playing the Judas to the Lord's memory. Paul sternly adds that the reason some of them are weak and ill and others have died is their misconduct at the Lord's Supper (I Cor. 11:30).

Therefore, Paul counsels the Corinthians to wait for one another. If some member is hungry and feels that he cannot hold out, let him eat at home before he comes. The Lord's table is not a trough where the gluttons get all they can while the weaker members take what is left. The meal is primarily a spiritual experience at which the Lord is host. The behavior of the guests is to be in keeping with His spirit.

There is little danger in the contemporary church of the Corinthian abuses of the Lord's Supper. But Paul's deeper emphasis on good taste and order in the services of worship is forever relevant. We must never identify piety with sloppiness. Form is to worship what good manners are to social life. We owe to God and to the memory of Christ outward as well as inward marks of reverence.

THE USE OF SPIRITUAL GIFTS. Read I Corinthians 12:1-31 and 14:1-40. Another problem was disturbing the peace of the Corinthian Church. Some of the members were "speaking in tongues," bursting out in ecstatic cries during the church services. Two evils ensued. The obvious result was confusion. While one was speaking another would be seized by a sudden frenzy of emotion and would pour out a flood of inarticulate sounds. Bedlam reigned. The second evil effect arose as a result of the evaluation which the church at Corinth put on these hysterical outbursts. The emotionalists insisted that their frenzies were the highest work of the Spirit. They looked down long noses of disdain at ordinary folks whose piety was less boisterous than their own. They made the point which the Ranters, the Jumpers, and their like have always made: that the more unnatural an occurrence is, the more it is divine. What was Paul's advice?

The Apostle's first reply to the fanatics is the reminder that the Spirit of God manifests itself in many forms; see I Corinthians 12:8-28: in the gifts of communication, of knowledge of divine things (12:8), faith, the power to heal (12:9), the ability to work miracles, to preach, to distinguish between *bona fide* and false spiritual manifestations (12:10), as well as in ecstatic speech and its interpretation. The one Spirit expresses itself in several ways, as one life pulses through many organs of the body. Just as the foot, even though it is not the hand, belongs to the body, so each of the spiritual gifts is legitimate, though each differs (12:15-16). As the body would be the loser if it had only one organ, if, for instance, it were all eye, so the Spirit would be poor if it had but one channel of expression (12:17-19). As the eye cannot say to the hand, "I have no need of you," so the possessor of one gift is not to declare the worth of another gift negligible (12:21, 22). The members of a church are like the parts of a body: what blesses one, blesses all, and what damages one, injures all (12:26).

While the Apostle proclaims all gifts to be equal in the sense that all are derived from God, not all are equal in the sense of worth, just as all the children of a family are equally descended from the same father without being equally intelligent or winsome. When Paul comes to grade the various forms of ministry he does not put speakers with tongues first, as they would have ranked themselves, but last! His order is (1) apostles, (2) prophets, (3) teachers, (4) workers of miracles, (5) healers, (6) helpers (servers of meals, financial officers), (7) administrators, and (8) speakers with tongues. See I Corinthians 12:28.

Two or three comments are in order here. First, Paul evaluates every gift on the basis of whether or not it builds up the church (I Cor. 14:12, 26). The reason he rates the witness of the apostles, prophets, and teachers so high and that of the emotionalists so low is that the former can be understood by the church, which receives benefit from their ministry, whereas the latter have a good time, themselves, but leave their nonunderstanding brethren out in the cold (I Cor. 14:2-4, 11, 13-17). Secondly, Paul is not opposed to emotion in religion—he spoke with tongues himself (14:18)—he is only insisting that emotion be under control, that "all things be done decently and in order" (14:40). Emotion is to a person what gasoline is to an automobile; there is no driving power without it. But what havoc a tank full of emotion can cause when the steering gear and brakes of intelligence are not functioning properly! Finally, what Paul is trying to suggest is that God manifests himself not so much in the abnormal —the ecstatic frenzies of the few—as in the natural expressions of reason, conscience, feeling, decision, sympathy, and speech. God does not appear so much in the unusual experiences as in the daily happenings of life raised to their highest power.

The Problem of the Resurrection. Read I Corinthians 15. While, as we have seen, most of the difficulties of the Corinthians were practical, they did bring Paul a theological question of the first rank. One of the cardinal tenets of the faith was the resurrection of the dead. How could the Corinthians believe that? The Hebrews always thought of immortality as a reunion of the soul with a body. The Greeks, however, looked on a body as an impediment to the soul. Immortality for them meant release from the bodily prison. How could they accept these preachments that the dead would be raised in physical form?

Paul's first answer is to reaffirm the fact that Christ did rise from the grave (I Cor. 15:5-8). The fact stands secure, however they may be bothered by the form it took. Christ had actually appeared to Peter (15:5); Paul had heard the story from Peter's own lips when he had visited him in Jerusalem. Five hundred lesser Christians had seen the Lord; most of them were still alive to confirm the story (15:6). James, the Lord's brother, who had refused to believe on Jesus during his earthly life, had been convinced upon seeing Him after the Resurrection (15:7). Finally, the Lord had appeared to Paul himself, a most remarkable event, since Paul was engaged in the persecution of Jesus' followers when the vision came (15:8). Nothing can shake the truth that Christ rose from the dead, however it may be interpreted.

This fact that Christ conquered death assures immortality for the race: "As in Adam all die, so also in Christ shall all be made alive" (I Cor. 15:22). Just as the soldier's victory means victory for all his countrymen, so Christ's conquest of man's great enemy means deliverance of humanity into everlasting life.

Having taken his stand that Christ did rise bodily from the grave, Paul goes on to reinterpret "bodily." Christ rose, not in the body which was laid in the grave, but in a "spiritual" body. The physical organism is, as the Apostle puts it, "a man of dust," "of the earth, earthy." See I Corinthians 15:47 in the King James version also. Its destiny is to decay and disappear, because "flesh and blood cannot inherit the kingdom of God" (I Cor. 15:50). In the hereafter the soul is clothed with a "spiritual" body, an organism which corresponds with its heavenly state in the same fashion as our present terrestrial body serves our animal life (I Cor. 15:40-42). Paul likens our present body to the seed which is planted in the soil; it decays, but out of it, continuous with it, comes new life. Similarly, we sow a physical body; it is raised a spiritual body (I Cor. 15:44).

Interesting as Paul's discussion is, the *how* of immortality is not so crucial as the *fact*. We can only guess what the afterlife will be. The kind of body that we shall have (the question which troubled the Corinthians) is incidental. The assurance we want is that our personalities survive physical death. The Master's triumph and the conviction that the fatherly God whom he revealed would not leave his children in the grave are all the guarantees we need. That God can be trusted to work out all things for ultimate good gives all the satisfaction we can ask.

THE QUESTION OF AUTHORITY IN THE CHURCH. Read II Corinthians 10:1 through 13:10. The final problem is another practical one. Agents (probably from Jerusalem) had slipped, like poisonous bacteria, into the bloodstream of the Corinthian church. They carried letters of introduction from Christian leaders, on the strength of which they claimed to be "superlative apostles" (II Cor. 11:5). They tried to stir up a revolt against Paul's authority. They not only questioned his right to speak for Christ (II Cor. 10:7), but assailed his moral character, impugning his honesty and that of his associates (II Cor. 12:16-18) and insinuating that the reason he had never accepted support from the Corinthian Church (II Cor. 12:13-15) was that he had obtained by "guile" what he had refused as a gift.

They contrasted what they regarded as bluster in his letters with his weak bodily presence and unimpressive speech (10:9-10). They said that the visions he boasted of were signs that he was mad (II Cor. 11:16, 12:11), and regarded the illness which had seized him on his short visit to them as a divine punishment (12:7). They were leading the Corinthians in a full-scale revolt against the Apostle's right to rule the church.

Paul's answer is a vigorous presentation of his credentials. First, he says he has a right to speak, because it was he who first brought the gospel to them (II Cor. 10:14). He has seniority. He it was who had betrothed the Corinthian Church to Christ (11:2).

Secondly, he has the authority which goes with firsthand knowledge of the gospel. The Apostle concedes that he may be a poor speaker, but has no doubt that he knows what he is talking about! (11:5-6). As regards the central truths of the faith and their relation to this life and that which is to come, he can speak with conviction. He had been trained and inspired by the Lord himself. He had been favored more than most men with visions and revelations. Even in times of greatest helplessness he is conscious of a divine presence which lifts him up (12:1-11).

In the third place, the Apostle reminds his critics that he has paid his own way. His ministry to the Corinthians cost them nothing. He had actually taken from other churches his maintenance in order to serve them gratuitously. He had not sponged on them. His necessities had been fully supplied by the brethren of Macedonia (II Cor. 11:7-9). Putting the whole matter at the crassest level, can a church look a gift horse in the mouth?

Once more, the sacrifices he had made for Christ and the Church constituted a claim to their loyalty. Read again that moving recital of his sufferings in II Corinthians 11:24-28.

The troublemakers in the Corinthian church were like slackers who had sat out the wars in some safe retreat compared with this grizzled veteran of the front lines who bore in his own body the wounds of his valor. It warms the heart to know that Paul's appeal struck home and that they welcomed him back as their leader.

At first this dispute between Paul and the Corinthians seems to belong to the far away and the long ago. Actually, it is re-enacted daily in the modern Church. Because the Church is an organization it must have leaders, persons with the power of decision. Happy is the church which, when it must choose its leadership, does not fall for the smooth talkers or the streamlined "successes" of the world but pins its faith in the Pauline credentials—firsthand knowledge of the gospel and self-denying service on behalf of the Christian fellowship!

Admittedly, the picture which the Corinthian Letters give us of the Church is not a pretty one. The graceless bickering, the easy tolerance of wrongdoing, the gross offenses against good taste, the feverish strife for the chief seats are well calculated to destroy the illusion that "the good old days" were so much better than our own. And what is the source of the trouble? Selfishness! As long as individuals, in the Church or out, are concerned first of all with their own pleasure, prestige, prosperity, just so long shall we be plagued with these problems that divided the Christians of Corinth.

And what is the antidote to selfishness? Read the matchless 13th chapter of I Corinthians. Not skill in speaking, for speech in itself only adds to the din (13:1). Not faith, for faith apart from the right spirit is nothing (13:2). Neither philanthropy nor even martyrdom will solve the difficulty (13:3). The indispensable is *love—patient, positive, self-renouncing kindness.*

LOVE IS KIND (13:4). We treat the other man as though he were "kin." The Master phrased it, "Thou shalt love . . . thy neighbor as thyself" (Luke 10:27; A.V.) meaning (as we have already seen) not as much as oneself, but *as though he were a part of oneself,* so that we think and feel as he does. Hence, we are not rude nor resentful (I Cor. 13:5). The cat-and-dog life of habitual quarreling and mutual recrimination goes out when loving-kindness takes over.

LOVE IS PATIENT (I Cor. 13:4). It is unwavering in its devotion to others. It is neither discouraged by their failures nor embittered by their ingratitude or dullness. It is not irritable (13:5). It "bears all things" and "endures all things" (13:7) the way the rocks take the ceaseless pounding of the seas. It never ends (13:8); it never gives up in this life; it outlasts even death.

LOVE IS POSITIVE. It does not seek the good by the negative path. It never tries to hound or nag others into virtue. It does not adopt the John-the-Baptist tactic of the ax and the torch (Matt. 3:10). Rather, it "believes all things, hopes all things" (I Cor. 13:7) in the confidence that faith in men's goodness tends to evoke that goodness. Love never rejoices in wrongdoing (13:6).

LOVE IS SELF-RENOUNCING. It is never jealous, boastful, or arrogant (13:4, 5). A critic of James M. Barrie, the playwright, once said of him that, while he was full of the milk of human kindness, he rattled the cans too loudly when he peddled it! So even benevolence can become an exercise in self-advertisement. True love, as the Master suggested, is stealthy in its benefactions, not letting even the left hand know what the right hand doeth! See Matthew 6:3. Christian love is never disguised selfishness; it is not a paternalistic conferring of favors on others, with the promise that they will let us have our own way (I Cor. 13:5). Its eye is always on the neighbor's good rather than its own interest.

PAUL'S SOLUTION OF THE CHURCH'S DIFFICULTIES

1. It is to be noted that the "love" the Apostle is advocating is a moral attitude rather than an emotion. It is not mere amiability, nor is it limited to those we like. In the Greek language there are three words rendered "love" in English: (a) *Eros,* from which our word "erotic" comes, sexual love. This word does not appear in the New Testament. (b) *philia,* from which our word "filial" is derived. It means "liking," as we are fond of a friend. (c) *agape,* the word Paul uses. (a) and (b) are supercharged with emotion. But love in the third sense is perhaps best expressed by the phrase Dr. Fosdick so often used, "undiscouragable goodwill." It is the recognition of the claims of others upon us and an uninhibited giving of ourselves to their needs, whether they are personally attractive to us or not.

2. Paul is trying here to show how a person would live at Corinth if he were a Christian. We may believe that

Christ himself sat for the portrait in the Thirteenth Chapter of First Corinthians. Indeed, one of our best New Testament scholars has pointed out that, if every time the word "love" appears in the chapter, we substitute "Christ," it still makes sense.

3. About forty years after Paul wrote his letters another great Christian leader—Bishop Clement of Rome—wrote to the Corinthians an Epistle called *I Clement*. It is interesting to contrast the conditions reflected by the two sets of correspondence. There were still serious problems of church government, but there was no longer any report of sexual laxities, of fondness for litigation, of lack of modesty in women, of disorders at the Lord's Supper, which Paul had combatted. Indeed, the Roman bishop praises the Corinthians for their steadfast faith, the spirit of brotherliness and lack of malice for which they had become known! The leaven of love had been at work across those years, transforming that ancient church. Love's success in Corinth makes us confident of its adequacy to surmount any difficulty which may beset the Church today.

VI

THE CHURCH
AND THE FUTURE

VI

Tomorrow, and tomorrow, and tomorrow,
Creeps in this petty pace from day to day . . .[1]

Every age, every institution, every human being, like Macbeth, must eventually come to grips with the future. This holds not only because the morrow is ever in process of becoming today, but because our thought of the future determines our strategy of the present. Our feeling about the morrow sets the mood of today. If one's outlook on the future is grim it casts its shadow on today, while a happy morrow makes the sun shine on the present.

The letters which invite our study in this closing chapter seem, superficially, to have little in common. The two missives to the Thessalonians were the first to be written which have been included in our New Testament, while the Letter to the Philippians was one of the last to be written, composed at least ten years later. Yet each majors, from its own point of view, in the same ultimate concern—*the future*. The

[1] *Macbeth*, Act V, Sc. 5, ll. 19-20.

Thessalonian letters look, telescopically, on the great question of the end of the world. Philippians peers, microscopically, at the question of the end of man. The Church is concerned with both. A philosophy adequate to the close of an era; a philosophy adequate to the close of a life: these were the high concerns of the Christian community to which Paul addressed his final letters.

THE CHURCH AT THESSALONICA

Thessalonica, today called Saloniki, was "a city set upon a hill" overlooking the Aegean Sea. Capital of the province of Macedonia and the seat of Roman administration, it was an important link in the great military road which bound Rome to her eastern territories. It was an important trading center and was famed for its hot springs. In the Apostle's time it was the most populous city of Macedonia, perhaps numbering 100,000 persons of mixed origin. Paul's strategy was always to set up headquarters in a dominating city whence Christian influence radiated to the periphery of a region. His work in Thessalonica is an instructive instance of it.

Paul made the acquaintance of the Thessalonians on his so-called second missionary journey. After a successful ministry in Philippi, the Apostle traveled southward to Thessalonica, where the Jews had a synagogue. According to the Book of Acts (Acts 17:1-4), Paul preached three successive Sabbaths and proclaimed Jesus as the Messiah (Acts 17:2-3). This passage also suggests that he drew converts from three classes: from the Jews—probably the more open-minded of his countrymen, who were hangers-on of the synagogue; from the "devout Greeks"—who must have comprised the main group (I Thess. 1:9; 2:14; and Acts 17:4); and "leading women"—probably well-to-do women of the upper classes who showed interest in religion. Probably the bulk of the Thessalonian Church were working people and poor, for Paul supported himself by incessant toil in order not to make demands upon their hospitality. The faith of the Thessalonian Church burned with the brightness of a newly kindled flame. Their religious reactions were spontaneous and intense (I Thess. 5:19-20). They possessed an exceedingly warm community feeling, evidenced, as we shall see, by their fear that their dead would not share the resurrection with them. The Thessalonian Church, if not so close and intimate as the Philippian, was one of Paul's favorites. Its members were evidently very dear to him, and their love, faithfulness, and patience gave him joy. He repeatedly speaks to them in terms of highest commendation and deepest affection. See I Thessalonians 1:2 ff.; 2:13-19; 3:6 ff.; 5:11; II Thessalonians 1:3; 2:13; 3:4.

Paul had not been long in Thessalonica before his old adversaries, the Jewish one-hundred-percenters, began to hound him as a subversive. They had caused him grief in Antioch, Iconium, and Lystra. They found him out in this new city. They engineered the arrest, not of Paul and his companions, but of Jason, his host, and some of the new converts. The trouble in Thessalonica is memorable, because these Jews did not charge the Christians with religious deviation. They raised a cry which was to haunt the Church for nearly three centuries—civil disloyalty. "These men who have turned the world upside down have come here also, and Jason has received them; and they are all acting against the decrees of Caesar, saying that there is another king, Jesus" (Acts 17:6-7). In the eyes of the intensely conservative Romans this charge against the Christians was the worst possible accusation that could be brought.

The magistrates, however, seem to have been fair-minded. After examining the prisoners they found that they were not so dangerous as they had been represented. After laying bonds upon them to keep the peace they released them without punishment. While Paul was, thus, not required to leave Thessalonica, apparently he felt it would be wise, saving the little church continued persecution, if he were to go. His concern for the fate of the friends he had left behind did not diminish. He had scarcely left before he sent back Timothy, his aid, to comfort the Thessalonians and to bring news of their state (I Thess. 3:1 ff.). Timothy gave a most reassuring report of their faithfulness and their love for him (I Thess. 3:6 ff.), although he informed the Apostle of the existence of certain evils in the church.

THE LETTERS TO THE THESSALONIANS

Paul feels impelled to write them his first letter. He expresses his joy over the good news of their patience and affection which Timothy has brought (I Thess. 3:5-10). He praises the strength of their loyalty as an example throughout Greece and Macedonia (1:6-9). He refutes the slanders against his good name (2:3-10). Then he goes into a discussion of abuses in the church, which we shall consider in a moment.

This first letter has especial interest, because it is the oldest Christian writing extant. It is a primary stratum in the quarry of Christian literature. Written for a community which had only been in existence for a short time, it marvelously communicates the atmosphere in which the first Christians lived.

Apparently the Thessalonians, making a brave stand, were helped by Paul's first letter. But some fanatics in the Church, either misunderstanding the Apostle's counsel or maliciously perverting it, were causing trouble. So Paul sends another missive after the first to make his meaning more explicit. It is our II Thessalonians.

THE THEME OF THE THESSALONIAN LETTERS: THE RETURN OF CHRIST

The problem which was disturbing the good people of the Thessalonian Church was the belief that Jesus Christ, their Lord, was about to return to the earth. To understand their situation we must recall one of the abiding beliefs of the Hebrew people. From the earliest times prophets and psalmists had foretold the coming of a Messiah and a Golden Age. In the long centuries when the Jews were flattened beneath the boot of the oppressors, they comforted themselves with the faith that the day of the Lord was coming. The misfortunes of Israel would be reversed and the oppressing Gentiles would become subject to the chosen people in a New Age which would outshine the glorious age of King David. It would be a new era not only of golden prosperity but of righteousness. The wicked would be put down while the faithful remnant would enter into their full inheritance as citizens of the age to come.

With almost their first breath, Paul and his fellow countrymen drew in this belief about the Messiah's Advent. When they became Christians they simply transferred this belief to Jesus. Hence, we find Paul teaching the Thessalonians that Jesus had arisen from the grave and ascended into heaven from whence he will return in a flaming fire (I Thess. 4:16; II Thess. 1:7-8). At his coming he will test men's hearts (I Thess. 3:13; 5:23) and inflict everlasting punishment on those who do not know and obey God (II Thess. 1:8-9). The faithful, on the other hand, will gather to meet their Lord, join in his glory and the final victory of his cause. See I Thessalonians 4:17; II Thessalonians 2:1; and I Corinthians 15:23-24, 53.

And this great day is nigh. As Paul says explicitly in Romans, "You know what hour it is, how it is full time now for you to wake from sleep. For salvation is nearer to us now than when we first believed; the night is far gone, the day is at hand" (Rom. 13:11-12). The imminence of Jesus' return is assumed everywhere in Thessalonians. The little community is acutely conscious that it lives at the end of the times. The miracles which the prophets had foretold as the marks of the Messianic age are visible on every hand: men speak with tongues and see visions; many are healed of their diseases; others display superhuman endurance. All that waits is the consummation. The air is electric with expectancy. As we sit at the end of a summer day and watch the play of lightning on the darkening horizon and hear the roll of distant thunder, knowing that a storm is soon to descend, so the early Christians lived. They never doubted that the age would close and the Lord return within their lifetime. It was only a question of the day and hour.

We have a new appreciation in our time of the mood of the early Christians. For we live, as did they, under a sense of doom. The *New York Times,* quoting Professor Leo Szilard a while ago, stated that four hundred tons of heavy hydrogen contained in cobalt bombs would be able to destroy every spark of life on the face of the earth.[1] The nations walk on the thin knife-edge of annihilation, and a trigger-happy corporal has it in his power to push them over. The learned men of every land are one in telling us how precarious our situation is, though they vie in figures of speech. Toynbee, the famed English historian, likens humanity to a mountain climber perched on a narrow ledge: will he advance, retain his precarious foothold, or tumble to his doom? Spengler, the German, more pessimistically, says that humanity can only stand at its post and do its duty, as the faithful Roman sentry did at Pompeii, when the fateful lava descended. Sorokin, the Russian sociologist, deserting figures of speech for statistical figures, shows us that the twentieth century has been the bloodiest in human history. These pundits are saying in their own way what I heard a man on the street a while ago put in the idiom of the American West: "It looks as though we are heading for the last roundup!"

[1] William L. Laurence, "The H-Bomb Danger," *The New York Times,* July 10, 1955, 24:1.

Even if we do not accept the pessimistic appraisal of the future, certainly the signs are present everywhere that our contemporary civilization is crumbling. A famous English historian once listed five reasons for the catastrophe which overtook the Roman empire. Note how applicable they are to our own time:

1. The rapid increase in divorce, which undermined the sanctity of the home, the basis of human society.

2. Mounting taxes and the spending of public monies for free bread and circuses.

3. The mad craze for pleasure with increasing brutality of sports.

4. The building of gigantic armaments which impoverished the people.

5. The decay of spiritual religion.

Nineteen hundred years and a different thought-world separate us from Paul and his Thessalonians. Yet, we feel very near to those valiant Christians, too, who heard the death rattle in the throat of their age and peered anxiously into the future.

GRIEF FOR THEIR DEAD. Now this doctrine of the end of the times and the return of Christ, which Paul preached and the Thessalonians believed so intensely, was causing trouble. Read I Thessalonians 4:13-17. To begin with, it evoked grief. For Paul had taught that those living when the Lord returned might look forward to meeting him and passing with him into the new life. But since Paul's departure several of their members have died. What will happen to these beloved members of the Church who have gone? Have they missed their chance of welcoming Christ and marching with him into the glory of the *new age?*

Paul's answer is: Never worry. The Lord will bring with him when he comes those who have died (I Thess. 4:14). In fact, the Christians who have gone on will rise first (4:16). The dead will meet the Lord even before the living. The resurrected dead, the living, and a great company of assembled saints will be seized and taken up together, as in a chariot of clouds, until they meet the Lord descending somewhere between heaven and earth. The Greek word used here for "meet" really indicates a reception, a ceremony fit to receive royalty. The saints will give a reception in mid-air for their returning King and will descend with him to the earth to live forever. Comfort yourselves, says Paul, with these words (I Thess. 4:18).

MENTAL UNSETTLEMENT OF THE THESSALONIANS. But there was a second difficulty which had arisen in connection with this belief that the Lord was soon to return. Read I Thessalonians 5:1-11. It was mental unsettlement. The membership of the church was in the grip of nervous excitement. They were acting like ships that had broken from their moorings and were blown hither and thither by every rumor. According to I Thessalonians their agitation was caused by uncertainty "as to the times and the seasons" of the Lord's coming (5:1). That is, they were asking, How long will it be before he appears? And, what will happen before his coming? The Thessalonians were victims of the natural curiosity about details which always emerges when a matter of vital concern arises. There has scarcely been a decade from Paul's era to our own when some company of people has not been upset over the question of when the world is to end.

To those puzzled over "the times and the seasons" of the world's end Paul affirms that it will come "like a thief in the night" (I Thess. 5:2). The time will not be known by any mortal beforehand. We may have strong suspicions, as the householder may fear a burglary. But the moment when it will occur cannot be prophesied like an eclipse. It will probably come when everything seems in peace and security (I Thess. 5:3). As men taunted Noah and his family as they hammered on the ark with no rain in sight, so the men of the latter day will be overtaken by the end when least expected.

The moral, therefore, is to "keep awake and be sober." Christians are to be mentally alert, keeping a close watch on themselves, lest the Lord's return catch them by surprise. They are to be sober, not so much in the sense of avoiding alcoholic excess as of possessing the sobriety of men whose faith is in God and who do not allow themselves to be deflected from the path of Christian obedience by rumor or mass hysteria. After all, as Christians they are the "sons of light" (I Thess. 5:5). They know that God has appointed them to be saved, so that they should be able of all men to be steady until the Lord's appearing.

The second Letter betrays another reason for the Thessalonians' agitation. The word was out that the Lord had already come, and the church had missed him (II Thess. 2:1-2). The signs on every side seemed to say that the birth pains of the new order had begun. Perhaps the Coming One had returned to earth without their seeing Him!

From the text we gather that someone had sent out a letter purporting to speak for Paul (II Thess. 2:2). It had suggested to these "jumpy" Thessalonians that the great event was behind them. Like the bridesmaids in the Master's famous parable, while they had been engaged elsewhere the bridegroom had gone in to the feast, and now the doors of opportunity were barred against them.

Paul resolves this problem by declaring that Christ will not return until first "the man of lawlessness" has come and been destroyed (II Thess. 2:3-4, 8, 9). In this passage we enter upon one of Paul's most enigmatic ideas. We can only sketch in the broadest fashion the Apostle's notion of the "end." His view seems to have been something like this: Before our age concludes, a "rebellion" will take place in the form of a widespread and violent defiance of God (II Thess. 2:3). Associated with it, perhaps as its climax, "the man of lawlessness" will be revealed (2:3). Apparently it means that a man will appear whose nature is lawlessness, whose character is evil—a human being with all the characteristics of the devil. This "lawless one" will embody evil as Jesus incarnated goodness. His father will be Satan, as Jesus' Father is God. He will set himself against every form of religion and will actually pretend to be God (2:4). This Antichrist will, however, be held in check by the powers of goodness until there is a final outburst of lawlessness. Then the Lord will intervene and quell the monster of iniquity (II Thess. 2:6-7 and 9-10). The Thessalonians are not, therefore, to be deceived into thinking the Lord has appeared without their knowing it. Things must get far worse before they can be better. The Antichrist must precede the Christ.

DISORDERLY CONDUCT. In addition to the grief and the mental unsettlement which Paul tries to allay, the idea of the imminent return of Jesus was having a third unhappy consequence: disorderly conduct. Read II Thessalonians 3:6-15. Some in the Church were living in idleness (II Thess. 3:6, 11). With the end of all things at hand men were losing interest in their ordinary work. After all, why rear a family, or build a house, or sow a field when the Lord may come before you get the chance to harvest it? It seemed a waste of energy to work and try to earn money when at any moment it might become worthless. With nothing to do, some of them were even becoming busybodies, interfering in the concerns of those who did choose to work (3:11).

Paul orders these idlers to get on the job (II Thess. 3:12). Here for the first time is stated the great Christian principle that honest work is one of the elements of Christian living. Paul adds the stimulating injunction: "If any one will not work, let him not eat" (3:10). Idleness is an offense against society as well as against God. Let the slackers therefore go without food. That will bring them around.

To the community as a whole the Apostle writes, "Do not be weary in well-doing" (II Thess. 3:13). That is, the loafers may be neglecting their duty, but the industrious members must not neglect theirs. Paul himself had supplied them with an example: "we were not idle when we were with you, we did not eat any one's bread without paying, but with toil and labor we worked night and day, that we might not burden any of you" (3:7-8). This word of Paul's not only is an exhortation to the folks of the Thessalonian Church, it is also a shrewd rejoinder to the slanderers who had charged that he made money out of his missionary campaigns. Self-sacrificing industry is the solvent to most of the ills to which a human community is heir.

AN EVALUATION OF PAUL'S VIEWS

What comments shall we make on Paul's view of the second coming of Christ and the end of the world? The obvious one is that *he was mistaken*. The Lord did not appear in the skies and whisk the faithful to glory. Paul proved to be a poor prophet of the cosmic weather. The failure of his predictions—and they were shared by the other leaders—created a terrific problem for the early Church. Expectancy melted into disappointment; hope fainted into doubt; despair broke loose and cried in the words of the author of Second Peter, "Where is the promise of his coming? For since the fathers fell asleep, all things have continued as they were from the beginning of creation" (3:4). The brilliant exultation of the Church fell back again with dull weight upon their hearts.

The basic reason why Paul and his fellow Christians were mistaken is that they presumed to know something which it is not given to any man to know—the future. God has permitted us to know the past by the power of memory. Through observation, deduction, science, we may know the present. But the future, and what it holds, God has reserved to Himself. Oh, I may have a hunch as to what is coming.

I may make a shrewd guess. Occasionally I make a prophecy and strike it right. But *I do not know*. I can never know what is going to happen tomorrow with the same certainty and detail that I know what happened yesterday. As the Bible puts it, "Boast not thyself of tomorrow; for thou knowest not what a day may bring forth" (Proverbs 27:1; A.V.). Even Christ himself, when the men of his time asked about the coming of the Kingdom, replied, "Of that day and that hour knoweth no man, no, not the angels which are in heaven, neither the Son, but the Father" (Mark 13:32; A.V.). Therefore any human being—whether he be the Apostle Paul or a 1957-model millennialist—who claims that he can foretell the end of the world, claims more than he can deliver. We may excuse those of the early Church, perhaps, for their error. But after all these centuries of repeated mistakes in forecasts, no intelligent Christian will let himself be taken in by false prophets.

While Paul erred in the details, there are three great truths in his teaching, as valid now as when he uttered them:

1. *Whenever the world may end, a Christian will be found doing his duty.* Whether the world blows up in an atomic explosion in 1957 or winds up a billion years from now as the sun grows cold, a Christian will be honest, loving, faithful. Like the old Connecticut Puritan, who, on the famous "dark day" in colonial times, when men thought the world was coming to an end, arose in the legislature and moved that the candles be brought in, because he wanted the Lord to find him at his appointed task; so the

true Christian will not loaf, whether the time is short or long.

2. Whether Christ ever comes back physically on the clouds of heaven, *He already has returned spiritually.* This is the conclusion to which the early Church came. After years of futile peering into the skies, the Christians gradually came to realize that his return was not to be an aerial display but an invisible spiritual presentation to the hearts of those who love him. This is what John means in his Gospel when Christ says, upon leaving his disciples, "I will pray the Father, and he shall give you another Comforter, that he may abide with you for ever" (John 14:16; A.V.); see also, John 14:26; 15:26; 16:7). Paul's meaning is essentially the same when he repeatedly uses the phrase "in Christ." The Lord is not a glorified human being whom we shall not meet until the end of the age. He is present here and now whenever a conscience hears the call of duty, when a heart grows quiet with divine peace, when sympathy melts into tenderness before the vision of another's need. The real Christ is not a supernatural visitant who bursts bodily upon our world from without, like the mighty general or the merchant prince in Hawthorne's famous story; he is revealed rather in a divine quality inspired in us, as the natives of the valley saw in the beautiful countenance of one of their own the likeness of the Great Stone Face which God had carved upon the mountainside.

3. Whatever "the times and the seasons," we may be sure that *Christ will ultimately triumph.* A God who can create this world is great enough to control it. The Being whom Christ reveals will not fail nor be discouraged till He has

set righteousness in the earth. Confident of that, we can be indifferent to *how* and *when*.

One of our foreign correspondents tells us that on the night of June 10, 1940, when the Allies abandoned southern Norway—a night when seemingly the West acknowledged the war as lost, handing over Europe to a lifetime of servitude under ruthless tyranny—he stopped to buy a paper from an old man in Fleet Street, London. "Well, how does it look tonight?" the correspondent asked. "I don't know, sir," the news seller replied. "I never read the papers, because I know we'll win in the end." A Christian may have the same sublime indifference to the details of the future, because the victory of Christ is sure.

PHILIPPI AND ITS CHURCH

Philippi, to which Paul's final letter is addressed, was located in the province of Macedonia, Greece. While Greek in origin, so far as language, government, and custom went, it was a miniature Rome. In the neighborhood of Philippi, in the year 42 B.C., Octavius and Anthony won their great and decisive victory over Brutus and Cassius. In honor of the triumph the city had been made a Roman colony. Philippi is famous in Christian history, because it is the first city Paul visited after he had the vision of the man of Macedonia calling for help.

We are indebted to Acts 16 for the story of the founding of the Church. Paul's usual strategy had been, upon entering a new mission field, to locate the Hebrew synagogue and infiltrate its congregation. But evidently the Jewish population of Philippi was very small, because there is no mention of a synagogue. Instead, he joined his countrymen at a place of prayer on the banks of the River Gangites.

There are three main incidents connected with Paul's first visit to Philippi. The first is the conversion of a prominent woman of means, called Lydia, a seller of purple-dyed goods from Thyatira (Acts 16:14-16). She had probably been a Jewish proselyte, who became a convinced Christian under Paul's preaching. The second event took place when Paul cured a slave girl, whose masters were using her talent for divination for their own gain. The owner whipped up a mob to fury against Paul and Silas, having them jailed (Acts 16:16-24). The third event is the conversion of the jailer under the joint impact of a frightening storm and earthquake and Paul's kindly treatment (Acts 16:25-40). The account in Acts leads us to suppose that the Apostle's stay in Philippi was not long; but it is certain from the Philippian Letter that he remained long enough to gather quite a number of converts and lay the foundation of a strong church.

As every pastor of experience knows, each church has its own "feel," and some are more congenial to him than others. So the Apostle Paul found it. Athens would hardly give him a hearing; Rome was standoffish; the Corinthians were a problem church; the Thessalonians, volatile and intense, were capable of going in either direction; but the Philippians were steady, warmhearted, and generous. The Philippians were his "beloved" (Phil. 2:12). They were his "joy and crown" (Phil. 4:1). "I thank my God," says Paul in the introduction to the Letter, "in all my remembrance of you, always in every prayer of mine for you all making my prayer with joy, thankful for your partnership in the gospel from the first day until now" (Phil. 1:4-5). The Philippian Church, if we may judge from the meager records, was a family church, in which women held an important place, and was noted for its generosity, especially its support of the Apostle's work.

THE LETTER TO THE PHILIPPIANS

The Philippian Letter was written from Rome. Paul specifically mentions the praetorian guard (1:13), and he sends greetings from the saints in "Caesar's household," the slaves and freedmen belonging to the imperial establishment (4:22). His friend Epaphroditus had brought gifts to him from the Philippians, who were anxious for his health (4:10), and his missive is a "thank-you" letter or, rather, a love letter to his favorite church. It is permeated by an atmosphere of affection, unfeigned, undisturbed, and unwearied, which had been expressed on the one side by warmhearted sympathy and support, and now by the sincerest gratitude on the other. It is no less suffused with joy; amidst it there rings the clarion, "Rejoice in the Lord always; again I will say, Rejoice" (4:4). The letter is, as would befit its contents, personal, intimate, and informal. There is no trace of the studied and conventional style of the classical epistle, composed for the eye of the public. There is neither careful and reasoned method of composition nor an exact sequence from one paragraph to another.

Doctrinal matter is at a minimum. It is a tender letter from a father-in-the-gospel to his children.

The Letter to the Philippians is of supreme historical value, too, because it is one of our few sources of information concerning Paul's last days. The Acts of the Apostles comes to a close with the suggestion that Paul reached Rome, "lived there two whole years at his own expense, and welcomed all who came to him, preaching the kingdom of God and teaching about the Lord Jesus Christ, quite openly and unhindered" (Acts 28:30-31). Philippians, however, pens in some of the details: Paul's growing influence in imperial circles (Phil. 1:13); the divisions afflicting the Roman Church (1:15-17) (a common malady of the early Christian communities, as we have seen); the friends who were attending him in his imprisonment (2:19, 25); the ever-present Jewish troublemakers, who were dogging his steps even in Rome (3:2 ff.).

PAUL'S IDEAS ABOUT THE FUTURE: THE UNDERLYING THEME OF PHILIPPIANS

The letter is of further great significance to us because it is in all probability Paul's farewell utterance. The Apostle is standing before the ultimate alternatives of life or death. He had appealed to Caesar and had been brought to Rome. He is like a man sitting in a courtroom waiting for a jury to report. Will the verdict be guilty, or not guilty? Do the days ahead mean more service to his beloved churches or further imprisonment and death?

But Paul is peering beyond the question of his earthly

fate. He is confronting the question of eventual human destiny. The Apostle is looking out from the Eternal City upon eternity. He is praying that, whether his death comes now or later, his conduct will be honorable and that he will take the verdict of the imperial court in stride, whichever way it may go: "It is my eager expectation and hope that I shall not be at all ashamed, but that with full courage now as always Christ will be honored in my body, whether by life or by death" (Phil. 1:20).

Paul is facing an issue which in one guise or another confronts us all. Whenever the world may come to an end, it terminates inevitably *for me*. Death may approach at the close of an imprisoning illness or the lingering twilight of advanced years. Or, it may strike stealthily, like the thief in the night. It may come violently, as it did with Paul, or its visit may be as gentle as sleep. But however it occurs, with agony or in our unconsciousness, in tragic prematurity or as the rightful climax of our days, life ends. And the absorbing question is, How shall we meet it? Resentfully, like "the quarry-slave . . . scourged to his dungeon," or with the confident trust of "one who wraps the drapery of his couch about him, and lies down to pleasant dreams"? [1] Is Death an enemy to be feared, or a friend to be embraced? Is our personal demise to be regarded as a grim necessity or as an appointment with a Heavenly Father? Is Death a dead end or a door into a wider life? This was the universal issue confronting Paul as he wrote to his beloved Philippians.

We are told by tradition that, when the verdict went against him, the Apostle walked out with firm step along

[1] William Cullen Bryant, "Thanatopsis," *The Poetical Works of William Cullen Bryant* (New York: D. Appleton & Co., 1929), p. 23.

the path to the Place of the Three Fountains and laid his head upon the block, while the executioner's sword ended his dauntless life. What was the secret that enabled him to meet his death like a hero?

PAUL'S SECRET: THOUGHT-DIRECTION

The key to the mastery of the inevitable, Paul learned in his imprisonment, is in proper direction of one's thoughts. How easily he might have fallen into resentment against those responsible for his plight! He might have followed the advice of Job's wife and even cursed God, when he found himself shut up in a meaningless imprisonment while lesser men quarreled over the missionary task and needy churches besought his help. He could have groveled in despair as the shadow of the headsman grew upon his wall. But that way lies madness! Instead, he tells the Philippians what he had learned in the hardest school of all: "Whatever is true, whatever is honorable, whatever is just, whatever is pure, whatever is lovely, whatever is gracious, if there is any excellence, if there is anything worthy of praise, think about these things" (Phil. 4:8).

We become in the long run like the objects of our thought. The vistas upon which we raise the shutters of our soul determine the mood of the inner life as certainly as a scene in nature writes itself on the photographic film. As Dr. George Gordon once put it, "You give a week up to reading of the sin, depravity, sickness, woe, premature death, sorrow, the whole black and terrible side of human life; let that get wholly into your mind, and by the end of the week you are about as bad an unbeliever as can be found anywhere in the world; your faith is away down toward zero; it is at its minimum. On the other hand, let your mind be filled with the sovereign sense of God, your own soul victorious over moral evil and undefeated in the presence of physical evil, renewed out of the Absolute Soul, enriched, lifted into a kind of quiet and heavenly exaltation in your own life; let all the other souls that have had similar experiences bear their testimony in your mind, all conquerors and more than conquerors, through Christ, over moral evil and over physical evil and every kind of danger and the shadow of death, then your faith is at the maximum." [1] By managing our thought we control our inner states, and then out of the heart proceed the ultimate issues of life.

What were some of the things "true, honorable, just, pure, lovely, and gracious" to which Paul directed his thought, enabling him to be more than master of his fate? There are three especially worthy of mention:

GRATITUDE FOR FRIENDS. First of all, he thinks gratefully on his friends. Read Philippians 1:3-11; 2:19-30; and 4:10-12. He rehearses the fine memories that he owns, of the Philippians, to begin with. He recalls their sterling service on behalf of the gospel and himself: "I thank my God in all my remembrance of you . . . , thankful for your partnership in the gospel from the first day until now" (1:3, 5). He knows that their concern for him leaps the barriers which his keepers have erected (1:7). He rejoices over the gift they have sent him, which is a reminder of their former generosity (4:15, 16-19).

162

[1] From "A Lesson in Christian Belief," a sermon preached in the Old South Church in Boston, Mar. 21, 1926. Privately printed by the Old South Society. Used by permission.

He is grateful, too, for his colleagues who are with him in Rome. Timothy has served with him like a son helping a father; while others have been interested in self, he has put Jesus Christ first (Phil. 2:21-22). Epaphroditus—a brother in the Christian fellowship, a toiler with him in the missionary labors, a fellow-soldier in peril and conflict, and the Philippians' own messenger to his need—he is also with him (Phil. 2:25). The broad, warm fellowship of the Church itself is a bulwark against the morrow. So Paul "counts his many blessings," and it tides him over the hours of present deprivation and future uncertainty.

Grateful memories have the power to unlock the cell of one's frustration and ease the saddest outlook. A distinguished psychiatrist tells of consoling a young widow of his acquaintance. He was at a loss for words, because she had been so well matched with a husband of only a year, whose sudden passing had been a tragedy of the first order. The physician felt that he had only crumbs of comfort to offer as she faced widowhood. But she brushed away his laments. "Of course I miss Dick," she said. "But I haven't room in my heart for anything but thankfulness and gratitude to God. I had a year of Dick's love—a whole year of perfect happiness. No other woman has had as much as I. If I shall live to be eighty I shall not have had time to thank God enough."

> *I hold it true, whate'er befall;*
> *I feel it, when I sorrow most;*
> *'Tis better to have loved and lost*
> *Than never to have loved at all.*[1]

[1] Alfred Lord Tennyson, "In Memoriam," XXVII, Stanza 4.

Grateful memories are more than a match for adversity.

THE ADVANCE OF THE CHURCH. In the second place, Paul comforts himself with the knowledge that the cause of Christ and His Church will survive anything which may happen to him. Read Philippians 1:12-20 and 27 through 2:18. Imprisoned though he was, the Gospel continued to be proclaimed, and the mere presentation of Jesus Christ is to further the cause (1:18). God is at work among the Philippians (2:12-13); he expects to learn of their steadfastness if he is able to come to them (1:27-28). If he is denied that privilege and required to die, even his sacrifice will be a libation upon the altar, a crowning of their labors (2:17).

Paul goes even so far as to say that Christ's cause was progressing, not only in spite of his imprisonment, but because of it! His bonds are a witness for Christ; his faith and intrepidity under difficulty have made the Roman Christians more bold (1:12-14). Knowing Paul, we may be sure that he had even used his prison as a preaching-place to convince men of the gospel. Furthermore, though he does not mention it, because Paul was in prison he had to write letters, making a written message take the place of a personal visit. In retrospect this is one of the greatest blessings of Christian history. For Paul's voice is now stilled by death; we shall never hear his powerful sermons. But because he was forced to commit his thoughts to paper, we have the glorious messages to the Philippians, Colossians, Philemon, and Timothy, inspiring men to the end of time.

Here again are facts that should hearten any of us when the years of adversity imprison our powers. We may be sure that the Kingdom to which we gave the noontide of our life will go on, even into the night, when our work is done. To change the figure, God is engaged in a mighty process of reforestration in his Kingdom. When a giant like Stephen is felled by persecution, God raises up Paul. When Paul's time comes there are Timothy, Epaphroditus, and nameless faithful souls in churches across the Mediterranean world, who had grown up under Paul's spacious shadow, ready by the divine Providence to carry on. One need never fear that a life dedicated to the Church has been offered in vain or that one's cause will fail because its servant has reached the end of his pilgrimage.

FELLOWSHIP WITH CHRIST. Once more, Paul fortifies himself against every contingency by the thought that in life or in death he would enjoy unbroken fellowship with Christ. Read Philippians 1:21-26; 3:7-8, 20, and 21. "To me to live is Christ," he says (1:21). Christ is the inspiration of his life; Christ's service is the aim of his life; union with Christ is the end of his life. All the distinctions of which he might boast—racial purity, ancestral nobility, ceremonial straitness (3:4-6)—he has renounced (3:7) and counts as refuse (3:8), that he may thereby know Christ and the power of His resurrection (3:10-12). Therefore, if the trial results in death, Paul will be the winner (1:21), because he can depart and be with Christ in heaven (1:23). On the other hand, if the verdict is favorable, Paul will still be able to live to Christ—enjoy his Lord's companionship—in the flesh (1:22). He will be able also to serve the Philippians and the other converts (1:24). So far as the Apostle is concerned it is a tossup, because he will be with his Master, whether in the flesh or the spirit.

We moderns think of "eternal life" as in the future. We refer to it as "the hereafter." Not so with Paul and the men of the New Testament. For them "eternal life" is a *quality* of existence independent of time. Just as we do not measure love in pounds or bushels, or evaluate thoughts by miles or acreage, so "eternal life" has only a casual relationship with hours and days.

> *We live in deeds, not years; in thoughts, not breaths;*
> *In feelings, not in figures on a dial.*
> *We should count time by heart-throbs. He most lives*
> *Who thinks most—feels the noblest, acts the best.*[1]

"Eternal life" does not stand in contrast to time but to sensuality, triviality, spiritual isolation, sin. If we are in fellowship with Christ, we already live in the eternal world. Death is just an incident for that relationship with Him, a ticking of the clock, of which in our engrossment with mutual spiritual concerns we are scarcely aware. The men of the first century had felt themselves under the spell of a deathless personality; therefore, they never tried to prove immortality, for it was merely a continuation of the felicity they had known. Heaven was for them only the infinite sea into which the river of their earthly pilgrimage flowed so gently and irresistibly that they were hardly aware of the transition from one to the other. The Pilot was the same.

Paul was prepared for the future, because he daily practiced immortality. He felt the resurrection already in his

[1] Philip James Bailey, *Festus, a Poem* (3rd American ed.; Boston: B. B. Mussey & Co., 1846), p. 80, l.31 through p. 81, ll.1-4.

moral life. He knew that his real home was in the spiritual realm (Phil. 3:20). His deepest friendship was with one who had survived death. Therefore, nothing could happen to him or to the world in which he tarried that could discomfit him. He would have agreed heartily with Ralph Waldo Emerson, who, when a millennialist rushed up to him and cried, "The world is coming to an end!" responded coolly, "Very well, madam, we'll get along without it!"

The other day one of England's most distinguished Methodists, Dr. Herbert Butterfield, professor of history at Cambridge University, wrote, "Neither the difficulties nor the options before us are as modern as many people think." This dictum is abundantly confirmed by our study of Paul's letters to local churches. The problems of the ancient Christian communities are still with us as our challenge. The record of the options which they chose is here for our instruction. But most of all, the Christ and the Gospel which consoled the first Christians is our inheritance.

He who embraces Christian discipleship finds himself embraced by it in a fellowship and made adequate for any contingency which the first, or the twentieth, century may bring. As the great Apostle phrased it so eloquently for the Romans, "Neither death, nor life, nor angels, nor principalities, nor things present, nor things to come, nor powers, nor height, nor depth, nor anything else in all creation, will be able to separate us from the love of God in Christ Jesus our Lord."

BOOKS ABOUT PAUL
AND HIS LETTERS

> *Books in print may be ordered from The
> Methodist Publishing House serving your
> territory. Your local church, public, and
> college libraries may be able to lend you
> the books marked "out of print."*

ANDREWS, ELIAS. *The Meaning of Christ for Paul*. Nashville: Abingdon Press, 1949. $3.00.

ASCH, SHOLEM. *The Apostle*. New York: G. P. Putnam's Sons, 1943. $5.00.

BACON, B. W. *The Story of St. Paul*. Boston: Houghton Mifflin Co., 1904. (*Out of print.*)

BAINTON, ROLAND H. *Church of Our Fathers*. New York: Charles Scribners Sons, 1955. $3.95.

BARNETT, ALBERT E. *The New Testament: Its Making and Meaning*. Nashville: Abingdon Press, 1946. $2.50.

BARNETT, ALBERT E. *The Letters of Paul*. Nashville: Abingdon Press, 1947. $1.00.

BLAIR, EDWARD P. *A Study of the Book of Acts*. Nashville: Abingdon Press, 1951. (Paper). 65 cents.

BLAIR, EDWARD P. *The Bible and You*. Nashville: Abingdon Press, 1953. $2.00.

BOWIE, WALTER RUSSELL. *The Story of the Church*. Nashville: Abingdon Press, 1955. $2.95.

CARMICHAEL, PATRICK H. (ed.). *Understanding the Books of the New Testament*. Richmond: John Knox Press, 1952, $2.50.

CRAIG, CLARENCE TUCKER. *The Beginning of Christianity*. Nashville: Abingdon Press, 1943. $2.75.

DEISSMANN, GUSTAV A. *Religion of Jesus and the Faith of Paul: On the Communion of Jesus with God and the Communion of Paul with Christ.* (Trans., William E. Wilson.) New York: Doubleday-Doran, 1926. (*Out of print.*)

——————. *St. Paul: A Study in Social and Religious History.* (Trans., William E. Wilson.) New York: Harper & Bros., 1957. (Torch Book). $1.45.

DODD, C. HAROLD. *The Meaning of Paul for Today* (Christian Revolution Series). New York: Meridian Books. $1.25.

EDMAN, IRWIN. *The Mind of Paul.* New York: Henry Holt & Co., 1935. (*Out of print.*)

ENSLIN, MORTON SCOTT. *Christian Beginnings.* New York: Harper & Bros., 1938. $6.00.

FOAKES-JACKSON, F. J. *The Life of Saint Paul, the Man and the Apostle.* New York: Boni & Liveright, 1926. (*Out of print.*)

GETTYS, JOSEPH M. *How to Enjoy Studying the Bible.* Richmond: John Knox Press, 1946. (Paper). $1.00.

——————. *How to Study Ephesians.* Richmond: John Knox Press, 1954. (Paper). 75 cents.

——————. *How to Study I Corinthians.* Richmond: John Knox Press, 1951. (Paper). $1.25.

GOODSPEED, EDGAR J. *Paul.* Philadelphia: The John C. Winston Co., 1947. $2.75.

HUNTER, ARCHIBALD M. *Interpreting Paul's Gospel.* Philadelphia: The Westminster Press, 1954. $2.50.

KEPLER, THOMAS S. (comp.). *Contemporary Thinking About Paul* (An Anthology). Nashville: Abingdon Press, 1950. $5.00.

——————. *A Spiritual Journey with Paul.* Nashville: Abingdon Press, 1953. $2.00.

KNOX, JOHN. *Chapters in a Life of Paul*. Nashville: Abingdon Press, 1950. $2.50.

_____. *St. Paul*. (Appleton biographies). New York: Appleton, 1932. (*Out of print.*)

_____. *St. Paul and the Church of Jerusalem*. New York: Cambridge University Press, 1925. (*Out of print.*)

_____. *St. Paul and the Church of the Gentiles*. New York: The Macmillan Co., 1939. (*Out of print.*)

LAUBACH, FRANK C. *Inspired Letters* in Clearest English. New York: Thos. Nelson & Sons, 1956. $1.50.

MILLER, DONALD G. *The Conqueror in Chains*. Philadelphia: The Westminster Press, 1951. $3.00.

MORTON, H. V. *In the Steps of St. Paul*. New York: Dodd, Mead & Co., 1936. $5.00.

NOCK, A. D. *St. Paul*. New York: Harper & Bros., 1948. $2.50.

PERKINS, JACOB RANDOLPH. *The Emperor's Physician*. New York: Bobbs-Merrill Co., 1944. (*Out of print.*)

PHILLIPS, J. B. *Letters to Young Churches* (A translation of the New Testament Epistles). New York: The Macmillan Co., 1948. $2.75.

RALL, HARRIS FRANKLIN. *According to Paul*. New York: Charles Scribner's Sons, 1950. $3.50.

RALL, HARRIS FRANKLIN (ed.). *A Guide for Bible Readers: The Letters of Paul*. Nashville: Abingdon Press, 1945. $1.00.

ROLSTON, HOLMES. *Consider Paul*. Richmond: John Knox Press, 1955. $1.50.

_____. *Personalities Around Paul*. Richmond: John Knox Press, 1954. 1955. $2.50.

_____. *The Social Message of the Apostle Paul*. Richmond: John Knox Press, 1942. 1955. $1.00.

SCHWEITZER, ALBERT. *The Mysticism of Paul the Apostle.* New York: The Macmillan Co., 1955. $5.00.

SCOTT, C. A. A. *St. Paul, The Man and the Teacher.* New York: Cambridge University Press, 1936. $1.25.

SMITH, ROY L. *Paul Launches the New Testament: Thessalonians, Galatians, Corinthians, Romans* (Know Your Bible Series, Study Number Eight.) Nashville: Abingdon Press, 1944. 35 cents.

——————. *Paul Writes Scripture in Prison: Colossians, Philemon, Philippians, Ephesians* (Know Your Bible Series, Study Number Nine.) Nashville: Abingdon Press, 1945. 35 cents.

SPENCER, FLOYD ALBERT. *Beyond Damascus—A Biography of Paul the Tarsian.* New York: Harper & Bros., 1934. (*Out of print.*)

WOODS, CHARLES TRAVERS. *The Life, Letters and Religion of St. Paul.* New York: Charles Scribner's Sons, 1925. $5.00.

COMMENTARIES

THE ABINGDON BIBLE COMMENTARY. Ed. by F. C. Eiselin, Edwin Lewis, D. G. Downey. Nashville: Abingdon Press, 1929. $8.75.

THE INTERPRETER'S BIBLE. Nashville: Abingdon Press:

Acts; Romans, Vol. IX. 1954. $8.75.

I, II Corinthians; Galatians; Ephesians, Vol. X. 1953. $8.75.

Philippians; Colossians; I, II Thessalonians; I, II Timothy; Titus; Philemon; Hebrews, Vol. XI. 1955. $8.75.

THE MOFFATT NEW TESTAMENT COMMENTARIES. New York: Harper & Bros. $2.75 each:

JACKSON, F. J. FOAKES. *The Acts of the Apostles.* 1931.

MICHAEL, J. H. *Philippians.* 1927.

MOFFATT, JAMES. *First Epistle of Paul to the Corinthians.* 1935.

STRACHAN, R. H. *Second Epistle of Paul to Corinthians.* 1936.

SCOTT, E. F. *Ephesians, Colossians, Philemon.* 1948.

――――――. *The Pastoral Epistles.* 1936.

DODD, C. H. *The Epistle of Paul to the Romans.* 1932.

DUNCAN, GEORGE S. *The Epistle of Paul to the Galatians.* 1934.

NEIL, WILLIAM. *Thessalonians.* 1950.

PEAKE'S COMMENTARY ON THE BIBLE. Ed. by A. S. Peake. New York: Thomas Nelson & Sons, 1936. $7.50.

A COMMENTARY ON THE HOLY BIBLE. Ed. by J. R. Dummelow. New York: The Macmillan Co., 1947. $5.00.

SUPPLEMENTARY MATERIALS
Related to
Paul's Letters to Local Churches

"THE GREATEST OF THESE . . ." A Dramatic Worship Service, by Mary Clark Tipps. Woman's Division of Christian Service, 1956. Price: 20 cents. Order from Literature Headquarters, 7820 Reading Road, Cincinnati 37, Ohio.

ROMAN EMPIRE MAP NO. 4, *Showing the Journeys of Paul.* (Color) 27x21 inches. 1938. Price: $1.50. Nashville: Abingdon Press.

NOTES

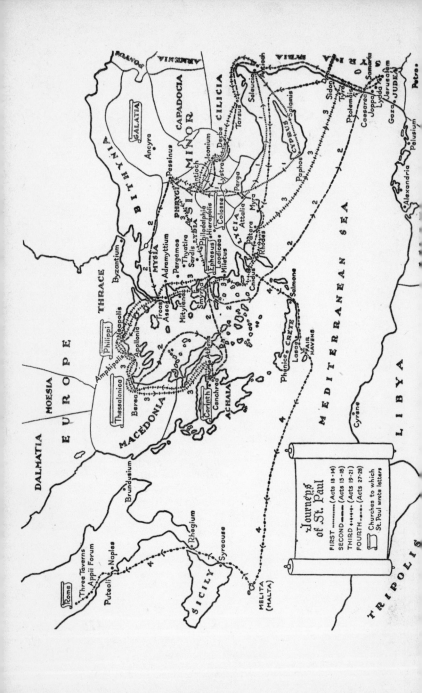

Journeys of St. Paul

FIRST .... (Acts 13-14)
SECOND ———— (Acts 15-18)
THIRD +++++++ (Acts 19-21)
FOURTH -·-·-·- (Acts 27-28)
☐ Churches to which St. Paul wrote letters